WOODEN IMAGES

WOODEN IMAGES

Title Page courtesy of Paul Davis.

NORMAN LALIBERTE AND MAUREEN JONES

Reinhold Publishing Corporation / New York

To Carol

© 1966 Reinhold Publishing Corporation
All rights reserved
Printed in the United States of America
Library of Congress Catalog Card Number 66-14435

Designed by Norman Laliberté
Printed by New York Lithographing Corporation
Bound by A. Horowitz and Son
Reinhold Publishing Corporation
430 Park Avenue, New York 10022, N.Y.

CONTENTS

INTRODUCTION

Wood has a long and glorious history in art. Appealing folk images have been created with it, and masterpieces have been painted on it and carved in it by the most sophisticated artists. Its role in the history of art probably began when primitive man first looked for materials in which to express himself creatively. This is a reasonable assumption, for wood was readily available and easy to work. It is a naturally beautiful material and can be found in a wide variety of surfaces, textures, and colors. Most woods are durable, lasting from several to hundreds of years. With a few simple tools — even a sharp bit of rock — wood can be split, chipped, or shaved to reveal almost any kind of shape.

With the discovery of various kinds of stains and paints, the artistic applications of wood increased. Juice from berries can stain wood permanently, as many a disgruntled householder can testify. Wood is also a good ground on which to apply most kinds of paints and was among the first painted surfaces. For the same reasons that wood has appealed to artists throughout the ages, it appeals now. It gives the contemporary artist a material he can utilize easily to express a wide range of ideas and esthetic concepts.

There is a certain rapport between any artist and his materials. This is based not only upon mastery of the materials, but on emotional factors that have nothing to do with technical skill. All materials, including wood, are inert. But the artist or observer brings something to them that is a combination of experience, intellect, and personal identification. Wood has an emotional appeal far greater than that of any other art material. It's hard to say exactly why, but there are several possible explanations. These, not too surprisingly, apply not only to the artist but to all people.

Wood is one of the few materials that come from living things. Modern man is surrounded by synthetics that are more durable, easier to use, cheaper, glossier, more weatherproof, and even machine washable. Yet most people want wood in their homes in some form — a piece of furniture, a panelled wall, a wooden image. Pieces of driftwood and chunks from trees and old buildings are commonly displayed as valuable works of art. Why? Perhaps because most of us feel slightly foreign if encased solely in concrete, steel, and plastic. Wood reminds us of life. Its surface is irregular, or imperfect if you choose. Its grain doesn't run with machine-like precision. It has a range of virtues and flaws. It pleases not only the eye, but the touch. It feels warm when you touch it. It even smells good. It retains the aura of a living thing, and its characteristics and irregularities invite involvement. Wood serves as a bridge with the world of nature; it is a nostalgic tie that is particularly appealing today.

On both conscious and unconscious levels, one finds wood a satisfying material. This book explores several ways of making wooden images, from the most simple, unembellished cutouts to complicated works of art requiring considerable skill. The chapters are intended to lead you toward an appreciation of what can be done with wood, with each chapter a stepping stone to help you understand, enjoy, and create your own wooden images.

— Norman Laliberté
— Maureen Jones

Wine Shop Sign, French (?), 17th century.

    The sign, roughly translated, means, "Let's go to the vine (drinking), with your wife's permission." Of course.

Hardware Store Sign, American, early 19th century. (Courtesy of the National Gallery of Art, Index of American Design, Washington.)

Isaac Fowle, one of the few early American artisans whose name is known today, carved and painted this sign in 1820 for the shop of John Bradford of Boston.

TOOLS AND MATERIALS

If you have ever made any simple repairs at home, you probably already have on hand many of the tools necessary for making wooden images. The following paragraphs list and discuss basic equipment. Basically the tools are carpenter's tools, with a few artist's materials included for enriching and expanding the concept of the image. If the information seems somewhat technical, it was intended as such. The equipment is the same for making a cabinet of wood as it is for making a work of art in wood, even though the intent is different and involves the use of two other essential ingredients — head and heart.

Wood

A few words about the kinds and uses of wood are important. What you make, how you make it, and where you plan to display your wooden image should be considered in choosing a wood. Say, for example, that you want to carve a delicate image in low relief and intend to display it outdoors. You must select a wood that is not only easy to carve, but one that will not warp or rot under the influences of wind, rain, and changes in temperature. If you plan to leave the image unpainted, you will probably choose a wood that has an attractive grain. If you are going to stain the wood, you want one whose color is sympathetic with the stain.

Your local lumber yard is the best source of wood. If your lumber dealer doesn't have the kind of wood you want, he can usually order it. Perhaps a nearby arts and crafts supply store carries it. Numerous craft, hobby, and home craftsman magazines advertise companies that specialize in supplying hard-to-find woods. Another not-to-be-neglected source of wood is your local junk yard or used furniture store. Large hunks of wood, which are rare today at lumber yards, may be available there in the form of old beams or railroad ties. Oak, walnut, mahogany, and other expensive woods may be salvaged from old door frames, chests of drawers, tables, etc. However, before you go on a treasure hunt for wood, decide what kind is best suited to your purposes. In most instances, particularly for beginning projects, the lumber yard is the best source.

Hardwoods. Hardwoods are generally close-grained woods derived from trees in temperate climates. Familiar hardwoods include oak, maple, hickory, ash, dogwood, black walnut, sycamore, birch, mahogany, walnut, maple, cherry, ebony, sandalwood, boxwood, pear, rosewood, and satinwood. These woods are excellent for carving, as their close grain inhibits splitting and splintering. Some, like mahogany, teak, and ebony, should only be used indoors because they tend to rot easily. Others, like oak and hickory, stand up well under most weather conditions.

Softwoods. The grain of these woods is usually large and open, and many kinds have knotholes and other irregularities to be avoided. These woods are easy to saw but are not advisable for intricate carving because their open grain encourages splitting and splintering. Softwoods include pine, fir, beech, elm, basswood, cypress, butternut, redwood, hemlock, chestnut, spruce, cottonwood, and, of course, balsa. Some, like beech, elm, and hemlock, are likely to decay fairly rapidly. Others, like redwood, are excellent for outdoors.

Light woods. This term refers to the natural color of the wood. If you are going to stain or dye the wood, generally the lighter the natural color the better. The reason for this is obvious: greater control in predicting the resulting color. Woods that are light in color are basswood, white pine, white oak, beech, holly, sycamore, and chestnut.

Dark woods. Dark colored woods are preferable for some projects, particularly if the natural beauty of the wood is to be an important aspect of the image. Many of these woods are so richly beautiful that no artificial surface embellishment is necessary. Redwood (sequoia), red cedar, and mahogany are reddish in color. Rosewood ranges from light red to deep purple, and walnut may be dark brown. Teak is brown with darker streaks, and ebony is black.

Plywood. Plywood is composed of thin layers of wood glued together. It is adequate for images shaped only by sawing. It is better for thin images than a thin plank because plywood warps less readily. For large, flat images plywood is excellent. In fact, plywood may be the only wood available in a size large enough to suit your needs.

Plywood may sound like the ideal, all-purpose wood, but it does have drawbacks. It is not beautiful to look at or touch. It is very difficult to carve

successfully. Its layers are set cross-grain to one another, which makes sharp, clean cuts with a knife or chisel practically impossible. The glue is also hard to cut into and chips readily, taking along slivers of wood.

Cutting Tools

A saw is essential for making most wooden images. The common carpenter's hand saw is good for making straight cuts. However, it is hard to use in sawing contours because the blade is broad. A narrow-bladed saw, such as a keyhole saw, is usually also necessary for making most kinds of wooden images. The name keyhole suggests how maneuverable this saw is. The tool was originally designed for cutting keyholes in doors, but is excellent for reaching and sawing most other kinds of hard-to-get-at areas. It is also handy in making interior cuts. If, for example, you wish to cut a triangle of wood from the center of a plank, you first drill a hole large enough to insert the blade, and then cut away.

Another good saw for contour and interior cuts is a coping saw. The handle of this saw has a C-shaped metal extension within which the blade is clamped. The blade of a coping saw is one-eighth inch wide, much narrower than that of the keyhole saw. A small hole can be drilled, and the blade inserted through the hole, then clamped into the handle. The drawback in this kind of saw is that the relationship of the blade to the handle prevents making deep cuts. The saw is best used for notching wood and for sawing thin sheets of wood.

Paring and Shaping Tools

A saw is good for rough outlines and shapes, but other tools are needed if the image is to be carved or otherwise shaped. Many kinds of complex carpentry tools are available, but we advise that you learn to

improvise with two very simple tools, the knife and the chisel. These tools are easy to master with a little practice and quite satisfying to use.

If the side of a plank is to be rounded or some kind of figure or design to be carved, a good, sharp knife is more than adequate. Any knife will do; an ordinary penknife can be used to reveal almost any shape. The trick in whittling, for this is what it is, is gradually to pare away the wood to form the shape. Don't try to chip the wood away; deep cuts may cause the wood to split. Whittling or carving away a large area of wood with a penknife, although possible, is just not practical. Most sculptors in wood prefer a chisel. Chisels are metal tools whose cutting edge is at the end of the blade. Chisels range from one-eighth inch to two inches wide. If intricate carving is planned, the narrower widths are preferable. The wide blade is good for large shaving and shaping chores. It is important to buy a good chisel. The cutting edge of cheap chisels chips easily and is hard to sharpen, and chisels need frequent resharpening.

A chisel is held like an ice pick, firmly in the fist, and driven into the wood with a mallet. The idea is to angle the chisel into the wood so that a shaving, not a chunk, is removed. Angling a chisel straight down usually cracks the wood. With a little practice, the beginner can learn easily how to angle the chisel and how deeply to drive it into the wood.

Incising Tools

Shallow lines may be cut into or scooped out of wood with several tools. Scraping a sharp nail across a plank will incise accents or details. Printmaker's gouges, used in scooping out slivers of linoleum or wood to make relief printing blocks, can also be used in much the same way in making wooden images. One particularly handy tool is the Dremel tool, an electric inciser with interchangeable points that range up to one-fourth inch in diameter. The tool is not too expensive, and can be purchased in hardware and hobby stores and art supply shops. Because it makes the task of incising lines quick and easy, it is strongly recommended for those who become enthusiastically caught up in the making of wooden images.

Smoothing Materials

When a smooth, even surface is desired, the area can be sanded. Sandpapers come in very rough textures for initial sanding operations and range through various grades up to emery papers, which produce an almost satin finish.

The kind of wood used affects how well it can be smoothed with sandpaper. The closer the grain of the wood, the easier it is to get a smooth surface. Some parts of wide-grained woods sand away more easily than others. This is particularly a problem if using an electric sanding machine; instead of a smooth, even surface you get a bumpy one full of ridges and valleys. Also, some woods — both fine-grained and wide-grained — are so delicate that hard sanding with rough paper will mar them. A little experience will serve as your best guide in what and how to sand.

Power Tools

If you can afford them, power tools are marvelous. However, they are not necessary; masterpieces in wood were produced long before the invention of power tools, and still are.

The handiest power tool is probably the band saw. This is a narrow-bladed saw ideal for cutting contours, notches, and trimming. The sawing table, which is part of the machine, can be tilted on most machines to get any cutting angle.

Another useful electric saw is the sabre saw. It is small and light enough to be held in the hand. Its blade is pointed and sharp, enabling the saw to start its own hole. This saw is not very expensive; one famous mail order house lists a home craftsman's model for under fifteen dollars. In saving time and energy, the money is well spent.

The modern electric drill, which is also relatively inexpensive, can be fitted with a number of very handy attachments, including sanding and polishing devices. These may be more useful in making wooden images than the drill bits themselves.

Glues, Nails, and Screws

More than likely your wooden image may be composed of parts that must somehow be fastened together. The best material for fastening together small, light pieces is glue. Glue is quick, easy to use, and neat. Many modern glues, including the casein glues, grip well and are water resistant, an important feature if the image is designed for outdoor display.

In addition to fastening joints, glue is important in another way. Formerly one could buy large blocks of wood for sculpting and carving. Today, large blocks of wood are almost impossible to find. The sculptor of wood has to put planks together to form his own block. This is best done with glue, as nailing or screwing binds together only those spots where the nail or screw is inserted. To find the best kind of glue for this and other special purposes, consult your local hardware dealer or art supply clerk. He will recommend the latest and most effective brand.

The classic, and the quickest, way to fasten pieces of wood together is to nail them.

Sometimes this method is quite adequate; at other times it is not only inadequate but inappropriate. A skillful carpenter can use nails almost anywhere for almost any purpose. The amateur wood worker, however, should use nails cautiously.

In order to conceal nails used in constructing a wooden image, they must be driven completely into the wood. This means that "finish" nails should be used. The head of a finish nail is not much wider than the shank. The head is also slightly indented, which permits sinking the nail into the wood so that the head does not protrude. This is done by fitting either another nail or the simple tool called a nail set into the recess in the head and hitting the sinking tool until the nail is deep in the wood. The small hole remaining can be filled with plastic wood. When the plastic wood has been sanded smooth it is difficult to locate where the nail was set.

The size of a nail is important. Nails too broad for the size or texture of the plank will split it. Nails that are longer than the combined width of the pieces to be fastened together will have to be cut or bent, an unattractive and unnecessary prospect. If your wooden image is to be set outdoors, get galvanized nails. The others quickly rust and break. Buy your nails where you buy your wood; the lumberman

Ship's Figurehead, American, early 19th century. (Courtesy of the National Gallery of Art, Index of American Design, Washington.)

Figurehead from a schooner built about 1815 in Haverhill, New Hampshire and sailed out of Salem, Massachusetts. (Courtesy of the National Gallery of Art, Index of American Design, Washington.)

will give you the size and kind appropriate to your needs.

If you need a really secure binding, use screws. Any part of an image on which weight will be placed should be screwed down. Boards that have been screwed together are much more difficult to separate than those simply nailed together; try and see.

Color

You may want to color your wooden image, all over or in certain areas, to enrich a surface or to create accents. There are several ways to color an area, but we will limit ourselves here to the most common. Other methods will be discussed as they appear in the text.

Enamels

Enamels are opaque paints which flow into a smooth coat over the surface of the wood. They dry either with a glossy appearance or a flat, non-glossy look, depending on the type you buy. Enamels come in small or large cans and in many colors which can be easily mixed to create an even greater palette.

Enamels are oil-base paints. As such, they may be thinned with paint thinner or turpentine, and these agents are usually required to clean the brushes used to apply them. Enamels, even the fast drying ones, take a while to dry. Once set, they are sturdy and endure well under most weather conditions.

Other House Paints

Today the range in color, finish, and type of household paints is vast. For this reason we shall mention only a few; your paint store can supply further suggestions and details.

Latex paints give a fine, smooth finish and can be thinned with water. This makes wiping up spills and cleaning brushes easy. Once dry, latex paints are quite hardy and can be washed.

Several kinds of oil-base paints are excellent sealers; that is, they will protect as well as beautify for a long time. One problem with these and most other household paints is that they come in very large containers; usually a quart is the smallest size. You may get around this by buying small tubes of concentrated colors that are mixed with flat white to get the colored paints. Then the only large container you need buy is one of white paint.

Artist's Oil Paints

Artists have been painting on wood with oil paints for hundreds of years. These paints should not be applied directly on untreated wood. Because oils tend to be absorbed by wood, the wood should be first prepared by sealing it with shellac or some other preservative or by applying gesso or some other ground on which to work. The painted wooden image, like a painting on canvas, should be kept indoors.

Artist's oils have another important use — the imaginative staining of wood in various hues. You can get a wide variety of rich, subtle tones by making your own stains. Mix the oil colors on your palette and then dilute them to a very fluid state with turpentine and a little bit of linseed oil.

Stains

Stains are absorbed by wood without altering its grain and character. This can be quite effective. You can buy either house painter's stains, which come in a limited palette —. mostly wood colors — and in large containers, or make your own stains with artist's oils, as described above. Stains tend to wear badly but can be fixed with shellac or varnish or waxed.

Acrylic Polymer Paints

These relatively new arrivals on the art market are excellent for creating a wide range of effects on wood. The colors are bright and stable, and the paints wear well outdoors. Used thick, they can be manipulated to give highly textured surface effects. Used thin, they are effective as glazes. Acrylics may be diluted with water, but once dry they are impermeable to water.

Inks and Dyes

Colored inks, various brands of marking pens and inks, and textile dyes are fun to use on wood. They come in a wide variety of bright colors and are excellent for making details. Particularly useful are those that come with a built-in felt tip pen.

All inks and fabric dyes will run on untreated wood, but on treated wood some brands work quite well. They lack durability, however; the colored ones eventually fade, even if coated with a preservative. Nevertheless, they are excellent for sketches in wood, and can always be touched up.

FLAT WOODEN IMAGES

The simplest way to make a wooden image is to paint one on a flat piece of wood. Some of the finest paintings in the western world have been painted on wood. Many made several hundred years ago are still luminous and clear in color and are sturdy. Some of them were made on rectangular pieces of wood. Others were cut into an interesting shape that is part of the composition itself. This is a unique advantage of wood over other materials. It permits the artist to treat the material on which he paints as an integral part of his design. A flat piece of wood, unlike canvas, need not be merely a surface for painting but can be used to extend or concentrate the total concept of the image.

There are three major kinds of flat wooden images: paintings on wood, cut and painted flat images, and incised flat images.

Paintings on Wood

Most paints are suitable for painting on wood. Some, like enamels and other opaque household paints which remain on the surface, can be used directly on the wood. Others, like tempera and oil paint, tend to sink into the wood or to deteriorate rapidly if not applied over specially prepared surfaces.

It is relatively easy to prepare a wood surface so that it accepts and holds paint readily. If the grain and color of the wood are to be preserved, the wood may be shellacked or varnished. Either substance must be applied to clean, dust-free wood and may be either sprayed or brushed on. Each provides a watertight seal and makes a particularly good ground on which to apply oil paints.

Often the artist wishes to obscure the character of the wood and simply use it as a ground. He may also want to work on a white surface, which allows a wider range of colors and greater contrast. If this is desired, the wood should first be painted with gesso or some substitute ground, such as a household casein paint.

Gesso is a chalky-white material designed for covering surfaces to make them better receive and hold paint. It comes ready-made in powder or paste form, or it can be made. Since the ready-made gessos are perfectly adequate for most needs, they are recommended. They are easy to use and can be diluted with water.

Gesso must be built up, coat by coat, on the wood. It may be tempting to apply a single thick coat, but the coat will dry unevenly and crack. The first coat should be very thin, about the consistency of thin cream. It should be brushed on in all directions and allowed to dry before a second coat is applied, in the same manner. Each coat must dry thoroughly, or cracks may develop as the damp lower layers shrink and pull against their neighbors.

Three coats of gesso are usually sufficient, and the gessoed panel should be allowed about two weeks to dry. At the end of this period, any cracks or other imperfections will have developed if they are going to develop at all. If the gessoed surface looks good, it will probably remain in this condition for many years. If a few minor cracks develop, you can smooth them out by rubbing them with a soft, damp cloth.

Gesso has one great advantage over paints and varnishes: it can be worked into relief. If a modeled or a textured surface is desired, it can be built up gradually with thin applications of gesso. While still damp, lines can be scratched into the surface or reliefs may be pressed into it for embossed effects.

No matter what kind of coating you choose, coat all sides of the wood: front, back, and edges. This is particularly important with plank wood because as the coating dries it tends to contract, ever so slightly. Even this is enough to make planks warp and eventually split or crack. When all surfaces are coated, the pull is evenly distributed, thus avoiding warping.

Stela of 'Ofenmut: 'Ofenmut offering before Horus. From Thebes. Egyptian, XXII Dynasty (?). (Courtesy of The Metropolitan Museum of Art, New York City, Museum Excavations, 1911-1912.)

Saxon Shield, Saxony, 1475. (Courtesy of The Metropolitan Museum of Art, New York City, The Bashford Dean Memorial Collection, purchase funds from various donors, 1929.)

Wood, covered with gesso, was painted by an unknown artist. The paint was probably tempera, as can be deduced from the sharp outlines and little modeling in the figure.

Inn Sign, "J. Carter," Connecticut, early 19th century. (Courtesy of the National Gallery of Art, Index of American Design, Washington.)

In the days when many people could not read, images painted on wood served as text. This inn was suitable for respectable ladies and gentlemen, as suggested by the figures in the carriage.

Tavern Sign, "S. Wadsworth," Connecticut, 19th century. (Courtesy of the National Gallery of Art, Index of American Design, Washington.)

Wooden signs were often repainted, sometimes because the establishment changed hands or, more often, because the paint weathered and faded.

Tavern Sign, "Temperance," American, ca. 1825. (Courtesy of the National Gallery of Art, Index of American Design, Washington.)

The figure (perhaps Aurora) in the chariot and the letters were painted in oil.

Sign from Toggenbourg, painted about 1702.

Tavern Sign, eastern Connecticut, about 1800. (Courtesy of the National Gallery of Art, Index of American Design, Washington.)

Artists and artisans roamed the countryside in fair weather looking for work, some of which they finished in their homes during the winter. The maker of this image was possibly Richard Brunton, a transient jack-of-all-trades — including counterfeiting, for which he was jailed at Newgate. The compass and triangle indicate that the Masons met at this tavern.

St. Michael, New Mexico, 19th century. (Courtesy of the National Gallery of Art, Index of American Design, Washington.)

Spanish priests brought their religious images from Spain to the New World. Naturally, as the Spaniards spread, the images became scarce. At first the priests made new images themselves, in the Spanish Renaissance style. Then the Indians began to copy them. As more of the work fell into the hands of native artists, the images evolved entirely new styles.

The Archangels, New Mexico, 18th or very early 19th century. (Courtesy of the National Gallery of Art, Index of American Design, Washington.)

The angels look rather like Indians, so one may assume that by the time this image was made, the artist had little or no contact with Spanish religious images. The figures wear Spanish soldier's clothing, a costume never seen on angels in Spain.

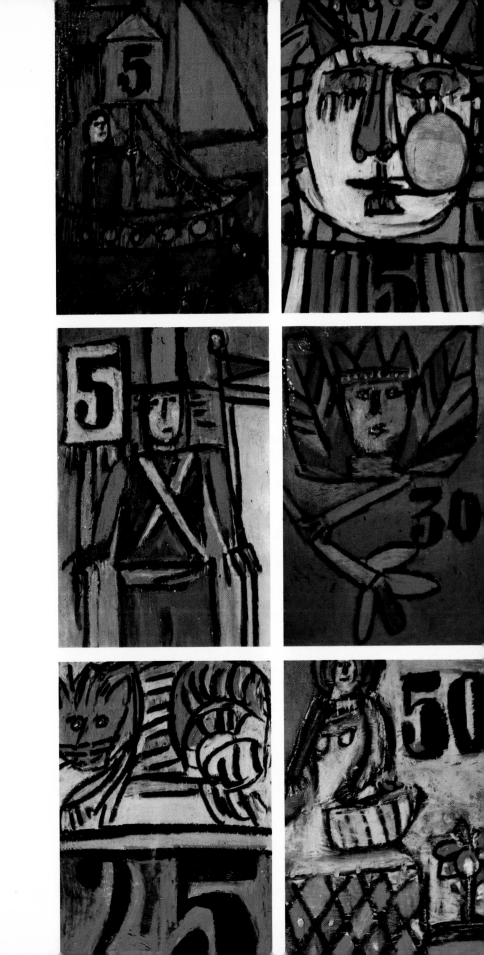

Wait by Paul Davis. Designer's colors on wood.

Cut and Painted Flat Images

One of the nicest things about wood is that, in addition to serving as a good ground for painting, it can also be cut. This gives wood a great advantage over other materials; it allows forceful accents and outlines to be developed quite simply. It also raises some design aspects that are not important in simply painting on a rectangular piece of wood.

Paintings on wood, like paintings on other materials, are intended to be viewed from one angle. But by cutting away an outline or some interior areas, you make an image with more than one plane. By moving slightly off center, the viewer sees not only the face of the image, but its sides. This means that the object is being seen, and judged, as an object in space. As a result, the image must be carefully, clearly, and — most important of all — inventively designed.

Certain design considerations are basic in making all cut and painted flat wooden images. First, the outline makes the initial impact on the viewer. It frames whatever goes on within it, so it must capture and move the eye around and across the image. Second, areas within the figure must be interesting, and the designer should recognize that as the viewer changes position, these areas change shape. Third, because cutting away pieces of wood may detract from any natural surface interest the plank may have had, the surface should be enriched so that it delights the eye. This can be done by coloring and painting details.

The best way to instruct someone how to design, cut out, and paint a flat wooden image is to make one for him. Then, once the basic processes are understood, the viewer has some kind of framework on which to build his own ideas. Therefore, let us begin.

Image drawn on wood

1. Keeping design considerations in mind, the figure is sketched in chalk or ink on a white pine plank. Next to be decided is how to cut the plank so that the assembled figure is composed of as few separate pieces as possible. Naturally, the fewer the pieces that have to be joined, the sturdier the image. Since interior details on our model project are to be cut away, the entire interior region should be cut out in order to be accessible to the saw.

The entire body, including the head, is first cut in outline. Then a single cut is made across the bottom of the body so that the saw can get at the interior. When this piece has been removed and temporarily placed aside, a short cut is made through one shoulder. Then at the bottom of the body a long arching cut is begun that will extend up to the shoulder cut. This removes one arch forming the body. Next the other side of the body is cut away from the interior.

Cutting the stalk

2. Once the interior section is free, we can begin to shape it by

further cutting. The saw pictured is a band saw. Its blade is narrow, usually ranging from one-eighth inch to one inch in width. This permits turning the material while working it and allows you to get the saw into small areas. Hand saws, like the narrow-bladed keyhole saw and the coping saw, are also quite adequate for this kind of cutting.

To remove the rectangular shapes accentuating the stalk, a cut is made along each flower down to the central stalk. Then a diagonal cut is made to free a triangle of wood. Removing this triangle makes room to maneuver the saw to cut out the rest of the rectangle. Each section is cut this way.

Forming the petals with a saw

3. Once the stalk is roughly shaped, we cut the details. Here the saw is shown cutting the petals. A single incision is enough to define them. The saw is hard to distinguish in this photograph because it is moving so rapidly. This reminds us of an important note of caution: Always be careful when working with sharp tools, particularly if they are power-driven. Continually watch what you are doing.

After the petals are defined, several small sections are removed to enhance the shape of the stalk and flowers. These are easy to make because, by this time, enough wood has been cut away to manipulate the saw easily.

Detailing the hair with a saw

4. Here the head is being decorated by cutting details in the hair. Incidentally, feel free to design as you go along. Just because you are using carpenter's tools, you are not working for the perfect cuts necessary in building a cabinet or a house. Spontaneous cuts can add immeasurably to the interest of the design.

Pieces ready for assembling

5. All the pieces of the final image are shown here unassembled. At this point they are fitted together and the image examined. Perhaps additional cutting is necessary. Often it is, for the original design outlined on a flat plank is now a free-standing form that can be viewed from many angles. At this point you can more clearly judge how your outline and shapes within shapes interact. Re-evaluate what you have, and design as you work on all stages of your wooden image.

Gluing two pieces together

6. After any new design considerations have been incorporated by sawing, the framework of the body should be glued together. Any of various wood glues can be used; your local hardware store carries numerous brands. The best kind of glues for this kind of work are the white casein glues, which are inexpensive and dry quickly, and come in easy-to-use containers.

Before you glue, dust the surfaces to be glued free of sawdust and any bits and pieces that will prevent a firm joint. As you fit the joints together, some glue may be squeezed out of the seam. Remove it with a damp sponge before it sets so that you won't have to chip or sand it off later. While gluing, take care that you don't accidentally glue the pieces to the work table as well as to each other.

Putting on dowels for legs

7. After adequate time has been allowed for the glue to dry, pick up the framework. If the glue has set properly, the figure should be quite sturdy.
When the framework has been glued together successfully, you can glue on dowels for legs. The diameter of the dowels should not exceed the depth of the wood plank; Dowels come in so many widths that you should have no trouble getting the size you need.
At this point, all parts of the wooden image except the interior

stalk of flowers have been glued in place. Why the stalk has not been glued will become clear in the next steps. For the moment, though, fit it into the figure without gluing it down. You may find that you cut too much away, so that the stalk does not meet the sides of the framework and therefore cannot be glued to it securely. This is easily fixed by dabbing a bit of plastic wood onto the short joints. When the plastic wood has dried, it can be sanded down so that it gives a snug fit.

Painting the face

8. Put the stalk of flowers aside and paint the image. The chalk used as guides in cutting may be wiped off or left on as guidelines for painting, whichever you prefer. In the illustration the face is being painted with dyes. These are absorbed into the wood, somewhat like stains are, and dry very quickly. We

recommend Dr. Ph. Martin's transparent colors, available at art supply stores. These dyes come in a wide variety of colors and are permanent. Enamels, oil paints, or various kinds of household paints can also be used, but they, of course, require time to dry and usually have a sheen.

Painting the hair

9. The whole figure is colored, even the interior edges, for remember that a free-standing form can be seen from many angles. The face, hair, and body are painted with dyes, and the legs are painted with gold paint.

At this point the reason for not gluing the flower stalk in place should be obvious; it is easier to

color the interior edges of the figure if you don't have to brush around a lot of complexly sawed details. Also, the dyes tend to run fairly easily. By keeping the elements bearing different colors separate, painting is easier. Once the shell of the figure and the flower stalk have been painted front, sides, and back, the stalk may be glued in place.

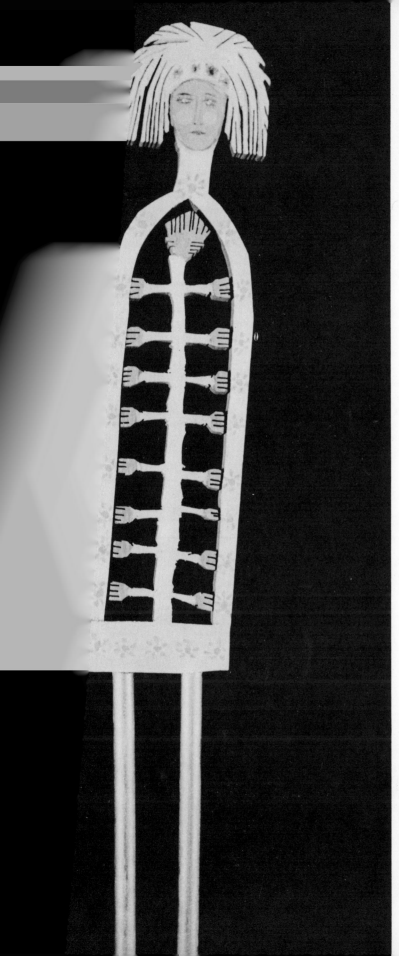

The finished image

10. Here is the finished figure. You will notice that the surface has been enriched with details. These were done with yet another medium, oil crayons. Oil crayons come in numerous rich colors that can be applied over most surfaces. They do, however, tend to rub off but can be fixed by varnishing. This not only sets the crayon, but gives the image a soft, pleasing glow.

25

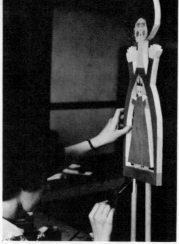

Painting the hair

This wooden image was made in the same way as the previous figure. At top left, the artist is seen painting the hair with liquid dyes. In the foreground is the box of oil crayons. From the number of crayons, you can

Coloring legs with gold paint

imagine how many different colors there are of these versatile materials. Another bonus is that crayon colors may be combined on the plank as you work for an even greater range of colors and effects.

The finished image

In the photograph at top right, you can clearly see why the cut-out spaces in wooden images should be well designed. The cut-out areas change shape as the angle of viewing changes.

Flight Into Egypt by Karen Eisin.

This image was cut with a band saw. Notice how this narrow-bladed saw can be used to make detailed cuts. The wood is redwood, left unpainted.

Weathervane, The Angel Gabriel, American, early 19th century. (Courtesy of the New-York Historical Society, New York City.)

Because sawing wood is easy, any kind of outline may be used in a wooden image. Here, a rather chubby Gabriel has been cut. Although the wood is flat, a rotund figure is suggested by the smoothly flowing outlines.

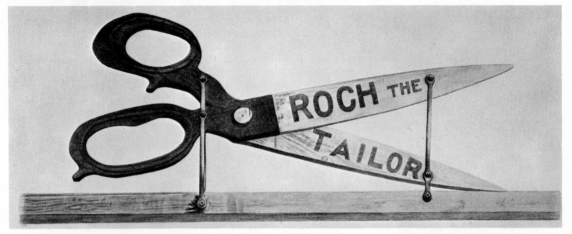

Shop Sign, "Roch the Tailor," Rhode Island, 19th century. (Courtesy of the National Gallery of Art, Index of American Design, Washington.)

Wood can be cut into almost any shape to serve any purpose. Because it was cheap, readily available, and easy to attach to almost any object, it had numerous practical and decorative uses around the home and store.

Weathervane, Mare and Foal, Rhode Island, ca. 1850. (Courtesy of the National Gallery of Art, Index of American Design, Washington.)

The horse and foal were shaped with a saw. Apparently a dark colored veneer, or thin sheet of wood, was glued over the mare. Notice how the head of the arrow was shaped somewhat as an afterthought.

Cigar Store Indian, Stillwater, Minnesota. (Courtesy of the National Gallery of Art, Index of American Design, Washington.)

This figure was cut on a six-foot plank, one and one-half inches thick. It was probably designed and made by the owner of the store, who felt he could not afford a manufactured statue. The figure is quite colorful; the clothes are dark red, green, and yellow, and the headdress is light blue, dark blue, and red.

Portrait Panel from a Mummy, Egyptian, 2d century. (Courtesy of The Metropolitan Museum of Art, New York City, Rogers Fund, 1944.)

When the days of Egypt's glory and fabulous treasure were coming to an end, burial equipment began to be made of common materials. This covering for a mummy was painted in tempera, on wood.

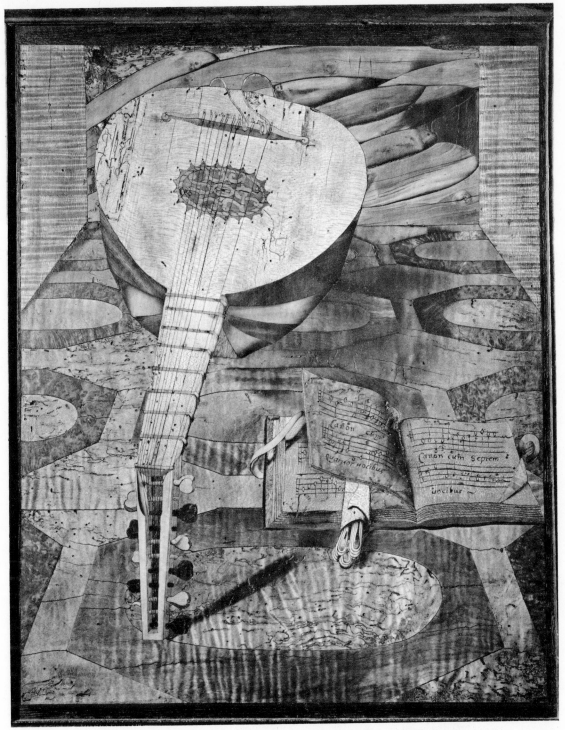

Panel from the Chateau de la Bostie d'Urfe, St. Etienne, France, 1545-1550. (Courtesy of The Metropolitan Museum of Art, New York City, Gift of the children of Mrs. Harry Payne Whitney, in accordance with the wishes of their mother, 1942.)

Italian and French workers specialized in cutting fine pieces of veneer and gluing them as a design on architecture and furniture. The technique, called *intarsia*, was extremely popular among those western Europeans who could afford it.

Incised Flat Images

There are several ways to create interest on a flat surface. There is coloring, already discussed, and breaking up the surface by incising lines into it. Cutting lines into a flat surface creates a shallow relief that can emphasize, outline, and clarify particular parts of the design.

Incising lines requires simple tools. The kinds of gouges used to cut linoleum and wood blocks for print making are adequate for most incised line problems. These gouges come with U-shaped and V-shaped blades, named for the kind of trench they leave.

There are minor problems in working with gouges on wood. Wood has a grain. It is easy to cut along the grain with a gouge but very difficult to cut across it. Therefore, gouged lines tend to be angular. It is quite difficult to cut a freely flowing, curved line with a gouge. Enough room should be left in planning a design for the irregularities in line that will occur with this tool. Gouges must be kept very sharp, as dull tools are hard to use and tend to slip, often because the frustrated artist becomes impatient as they snag on some simple cut. Since gouges are sharp, they should be worked away from the body. This is a good rule to observe when using all sharp tools.

A gouge should be angled so that it makes a shallow cut into the wood. Don't try to angle a gouge so that it cuts deep into the wood, as you are likely to remove a splinter of wood rather than the desired shaving.

An alternative to the gouge is the electric incising tool discussed on page 10 of the Tools and Materials section. If you plan to do extensive incising, you should invest in one. This electric tool is marvelous. It permits almost as much freedom of line as a pencil does. The following sequence shows one way of using the electric incising tool.

1. Punchinello, the Italian ancestor of Punch, is seen here astride a spirited if not very trustworthy steed — a chicken. The image has been drawn with a marking pen on white pine, and its amusing character has been emphasized by cutting it in outline. There is a lot to be done on the remaining flat surface: parts of bodies must be differentiated and large, monotonous areas must be broken up to add interest. These are problems that can be solved in a freshly different manner with an incising tool.

Punch, drawn and cut in outline on a pine plank

2. In this photograph the electric incising tool is being used. Its rapidly rotating bit drills along the wood, leaving a trench deep enough to break up the surface clearly.

The drill cuts down, around, and across the grain with the greatest ease, unlike hand tools. It works so rapidly that it can be used in a free manner, lightly moving over the surface following the inked lines drawn as rough guides.

Using the electric incising tool

30

The finished image, colored with dyes and oil crayons

Decorated Box by Anne Raymo.
Ready-made objects can be incised and painted. Here a small box from India was painted with tempera and drilled with the electric incising tool.

3. After the lines are incised, the image is stained dark wine color all over: front, sides, and back. Since stain is absorbed by wood and runs, there is no difficulty in staining the incised lines. The stain dries in a few minutes, after which oil crayons are used. The incised lines are too narrow and deep to be reached with the blunt oil crayons. This is all right: They were not planned to be used like the lines in a coloring book, but to set off small jewels of color.

French General.
The figure was cut from a pine plank, incised, and colored with dyes and oil crayons. It was shellacked to protect the coloring agents.

31

Cookie Mold.

A long plank of one-half-inch-thick pine was covered with flat black house paint. The electric scriber was used to cut through the paint to reveal the white pine beneath. Vegetable oil was used to make the paint more luminous and to prepare the wood so that the cookie dough wouldn't stick to it.

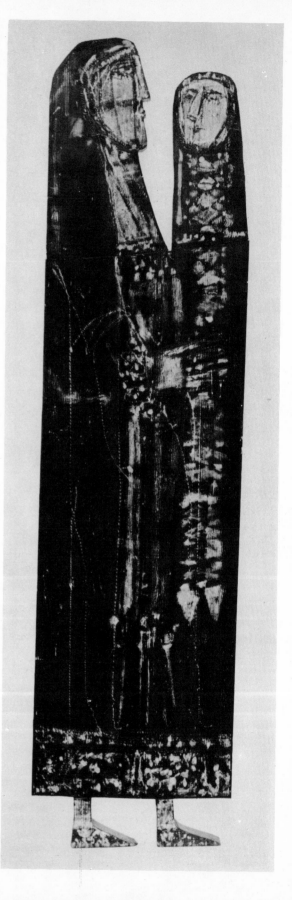

Mother and Child by Anne Raymo.

This is an interesting technique. The artist drew with pastel chalks, on a two-inch-thick maple board, then with a brayer rolled black printer's ink over the entire board. In the pastelled areas, the brayer picked up bits of the pastel dust and deposited them as tiny flecks in the broad, unchalked areas.

Wives and Lovers by Anne Raymo.

Three-quarter-inch-thick plywood was used to make these panels. Plywood is excellent for flat images; it is often the only wood that comes large enough for big images. The three panels — painted, chalked, and incised — were mounted in one frame.

Portraits and Profiles by Anne Raymo.

The human face and personality have inspired artists as long as they have been making images. Here four different people have been rendered in redwood. The natural quality of the material adds to the design.

Gypsy Wagon.

Away we go, in pine colored with paints and chalks. This jolly image may be hung on a wall or glued on furniture. No matter where it is used, its gaiety is a cheerful reminder of the footloose life — if only imaginary.

RELIEF IMAGES

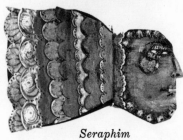

Seraphim

An artist makes several conscious choices in developing the impression he wishes to achieve. By simply deciding what size the final work will be he begins to set its tone. He knows what mass conveys, how line can be used. He carefully considers various colors, their combinations, and the effects they produce — accent, unity, impact. He also knows how the distribution of light and dark in an image can affect its emotional content. He may create the light and dark areas with color, or choose some form of presentation that physically incorporates dark and light areas. One such form is the relief.

In a relief image some or all of the elements project from a background. They may project slightly, or so much that they appear to be almost free-standing sculpture. The elements that project receive more light than those that do not. This naturally creates light and dark areas. By translating his idea as a relief, the artist physically builds contrast in his image. An image with physically distinct planes also has greater surface. This means that there is more material to catch the eye and involve it in exploring the image. The character of wood helps reinforce this; its grain

has variety and direction. Because an image in relief has dimension it tempts the viewer to perceive it with still another sense — touch, and here wood has an esthetic advantage over most other materials. It feels good. Unlike stone, the other classic material for reliefs, it is warm. It can be sanded smooth, providing one kind of tactile experience. It can be left rough, providing another. Wood can convey a range of visual and tactile impressions.

The two main ways to create a wooden image in relief are to build the image and to carve it.

Built-up Reliefs

This is the easiest way to make a relief image. You start with the background and build the image by adding layers of material to it. This approach gives you a great deal of freedom, as you can experiment as you work. If one kind of addition doesn't work, try another. If the other doesn't fit exactly, remove it and shape it so that it does. You can usually assemble all the pieces in place on the background, judge how they look, and then permanently affix them with glue, nails, or whatever.

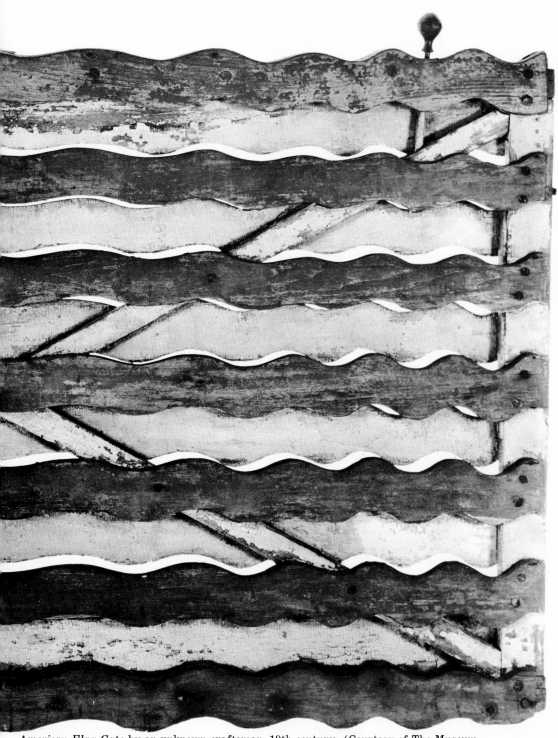

American Flag Gate by an unknown craftsman, 19th century. (Courtesy of The Museum of Early American Folk Arts, New York City.)

Because wood is so easy to cut and paint, it has been used decoratively for all kinds of purposes. The maker of this image, perhaps a homeowner or hired man skilled in carpentry, created an impressive and functional rendition of the American flag by nailing flat pieces of wood onto a ready-built gate.

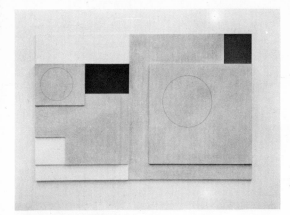

Relief by Ben Nicholson, 1939. (Courtesy of The Museum of Modern Art, New York City, Gift of H.S. Ede and the artist.)

The bold rectangular shapes of this image are emphatic. They are delineated by shape, color, and shadows cast by their different planes. The inscribed circles add to the over-all mathematically precise impression of this image.

Composition by Roberto Crippa, 1959. (Courtesy of The Museum of Modern Art, New York City.)

Bark is also wood, and can be used imaginatively in a wooden image. The bark shown here has fine cracks, a natural pattern that unobtrusively breaks up the surface of the strips. These broad planes have also been artificially interrupted by lightly contrasting divisions painted by the artist. The bark was mounted on plywood coated with paint and sawdust.

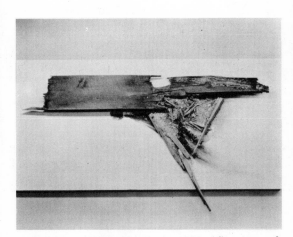

In Flight by Robert Mallary, 1957. (Courtesy of The Museum of Modern Art, New York City. Larry Aldrich Foundation.)

Carefully worked and polished woods are not the only kinds suitable for wooden images. Worn and weathered woods found on old buildings and fences and in vacant lots may also be incorporated into a work of art. Here pieces of wood and sand were glued on a plywood board. The resulting impression seems to soar due to the angle of the smaller fragments and the sharp contrast between forms and dark and light areas.

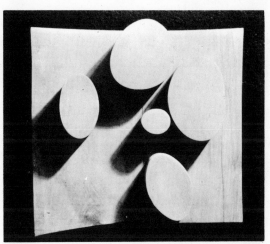

Objects Arranged According to the Law of Chance, Navels by Jean Arp, 1930. (Courtesy of The Museum of Modern Art, New York City.)

Wood often needs no coloring or other decoration to embellish it. Here natural wood has been cut and varnished to protect it and emphasize its grain. The shadows cast by the oval objects are an important part of the overall impression.

Seraphim.

A relief may be made by nailing strips of wood, one over the other. Here the ready-made scalloped strips sold as trimming by lumber yards were nailed on a redwood plank. The strips and plank were stained before they were put together, and details added later with oil crayons.

Virgin Enthroned by Anne Raymo.

Three panels of wood form this tryptich. The wood has been colored with dyes and oil crayons and incised with an electric tool. The numerous representations of the Christ Child were cut from art magazines and books. They were glued on wood, which was then cut to their shapes and mounted on small shelves so that the pictures project from the planks.

Panel, French Regency period, 18th century. (Courtesy of The Metropolitan Museum of Art, New York City, Gift of J. Pierpont Morgan, 1906.)

Wood can be developed to serve as a foil for other objects. The art work here is the entire panel, not just the painting. The carved oak embellishments add immeasurably to the over-all impression of the painting.

Toward the end of the 19th century, a way of softening wood and molding it into shapes such as those shown here was developed. The technique is still used today, and highly decorative pressed wood strips can be bought from large lumber yards and interior decorators.

The Stable by Bernard Langlais. (Photo courtesy of U.S. Plywood Corporation, New York City.)

Relief can be built up many ways. This entire scene was made with planks, angled toward the viewer to give dimension to the figures in the foreground. Notice how the strips form areas within areas; they were not all laid down in one direction. Some of the wood was left untreated; some of it was stained. The wood representing the field is old painted wood, battered and scratched to reveal the natural color underneath.

Carved Reliefs

Carved reliefs should be well planned, and a fairly complete sketch worked out on paper. Those areas to be cut out should be indicated by darkening them with the drawing tool. The dark areas represent shadows, and the dark and light sketch will help you estimate how effective the over-all distribution of high and low areas is.

Until you get used to handling your cutting tool and the wood, your first efforts should be simple in design and execution. There are certain tricks and a feeling of what can be done with the medium that are acquired only through experience.

When the design has been transferred to the wood, begin carving. Start in the least important areas; then if you make a mistake, the error is not too serious.

Use sharp tools. A penknife, X-Acto knife, or commercial wood carving knife can be used for most cutting chores. Some wood carvers use single-edged razor blades. They are cheap, and can be discarded when they become dull.

The idea in carving is to gradually reveal the image, shaving off slivers or cutting out small pieces, bit by bit. Forcing a knife deep into wood usually splits the wood.

Roughly carve the entire image. It is not advisable to finish one area and then start another. As you are cutting the block, you may run across irregularities that must be dealt with by altering the design. Or, the act of carving itself may suggest an exciting treatment for the image. Let the wood suggest its own uses as you work with it.

Lion Panel, Swiss, 15th century. (Courtesy of The Metropolitan Museum of Art, New York City, Rogers Fund, 1908.)

Elaborately carved figures in fairly high relief contrast with the flat, painted background. The designs carved on the lions, birds, trees, and flowers are abstract.

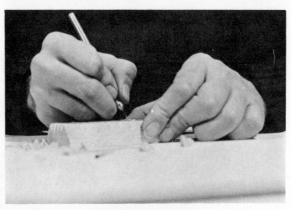

Any comfortable way of working is suitable for carving a relief in wood.

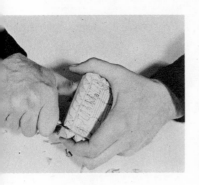

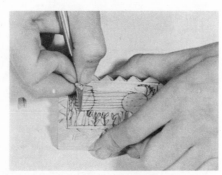

Lower right: Decorated Boxes for Jewelry, Memorabilia, and Old Love Letters by Bill Greer. Old boxes, found in second-hand shops, were refinished. Then small, carved reliefs were glued on them to make them more personal. The bottom box bears the relief shown being carved in the previous photos.

Pietà, French, Transitional Gothic-Renaissance, ca. 1510-1515. (Courtesy of The Metropolitan Museum of Art, New York City, Gift of two trustees, 1905.)

A great deal of Western art was devoted to religious themes. Stories from the Old and New Testaments have inspired the sophisticated professional artist working for a king and the peasant in his cottage. These artists had one thing in common: they were usually developing their images in wood. Here is an example by an unknown artist. The central figures have been emphasized by carving them in high relief, and the image has been painted and gilded.

←

Rosary Box by Bill Greer.

The entire image celebrates the mystery of the rosary. Many symbolic elements have been used to emphasize the function of the box. The spiky halo is exultant; the flowers and leaves, humble reminders of nature. Behind the doors is a small case for a rosary. This wooden image was carved in white pine and stained and waxed with shoe polish.

Mounted Knights in Gothic Armor, German, ca. 1450-1500. (Courtesy of The Metropolitan Museum of Art, New York City, The Bashford Dean Memorial Collection, Purchase funds from various sources, 1929.)

The knights, who seem to be on the losing side of a battle, are almost caricatures. They are relatively flat, both in conception and carving. Their bodies do not recede in space; most parts are turned toward the viewer. Yet somehow the image is quite realistic. The poses, even though distorted, give the impression that a moment of an actual battle has been captured in wood.

America, Bohemia, 18th century. (Courtesy of The Cooper Union Museum, New York City.)

Two frontiers, Africa and America, fascinated 18th century Europeans. Tired of one skirmish or full-scale war right after the other, they saw these undeveloped lands as Paradises on earth. Their native inhabitants were thought of as the innocent children of Nature, unspoiled by the decadence of Old World society. Here an American Indian, the Noble Savage, is drawn in a chariot by two unicorns, symbols of innocence. The strange, armadillo-like animal in the foreground moves trustingly along, side by side with man. The technique used to create the image is Eger work, a virtuoso technique of carving and inlaying wood.

Legendary Scene, Flemish late Gothic, ca. 1450-1500. (Courtesy of The Metropolitan Museum of Art, New York City, Gift of J. Pierpont Morgan, 1916.)

There is a great deal of depth in this relief, so much so that it almost looks like real actors on a stage. The story depicted is lost to us, but the wood tells a story of its own about what a Gothic town looked like — paved streets, tiled roofs, and barred doorways. Because wood is durable, wooden images often serve hundreds of years later as pictorial records of the times in which they were made.

Emblem of a Nation, American, 19th century. (Courtesy of the National Gallery of Art, Index of American Design, Washington.)

The noble eagle, defiant and brave, became the symbol of the United States in 1782, when Congress adopted it for the great seal. Since then it has appeared frequently in American art, and has been a particularly popular subject for reliefs carved to decorate functional objects like ships and stores.

Stern Board, American, early 19th century. (Courtesy of The New-York Historical Society, New York City.)

The combined eagle and flag image was popular on ships, and the symbol was carried over the seven seas to all corners of the earth. The representation of the eagle is more or less standard; the feathers were shallowly carved more as a design than a naturalistic depiction. The flags, on the other hand, are quite realistic, probably because they are more deeply carved.

←

Butter Mold, American. (Courtesy of the National Gallery of Art, Index of American Design, Washington.)

Here the design has been tailored to the use of the object bearing the design. Because this is a mold and its decor is to be transferred in reverse, the initials are backwards. Note the two representations of how the butter was made: the churn on the left and the clover flower on the right.

Mangle Boards, Dutch, 18th century. (Courtesy of The Metropolitan Museum of Art, New York City, Rogers Fund, 1911.)

The carving in these boards should be closely examined; it is truly magnificent. Each motif is different, not only in design but in the way it has been cut. In some, the light is focused into pinpoints; in others it falls in squares. Carving, and carving alone, was used to create a wide range of effects.

Medallion, Japanese, 17th century. (Courtesy of The Metropolitan Museum of Art, New York City, Rogers Fund, 1912.)

This medallion is the crest of the Tokugawa family. The image is composed of two basic geometric shapes, the circle and the triangle (formed by the water lilies). The design is deceptively simple yet powerful, probably the impression the family wished to convey of itself.

SCULPTURED IMAGES

Punch, Rhode Island, 19th Century. (Courtesy of the National Gallery of Art, Index of American Design, Washington.)

Although most cigar store figures were Indians, other personalities were also carved to suit the purpose. Here the humorous English Punch proffers cigars to passersby. The figure was probably made to order, either because the proprietor of the shop was English or because the shop carried some fancy kind of British cigars.

A sculptured image is three dimensional. It has front, back, sides, top and bottom. It is free standing, not projecting from, or part of, any background. In other words, a sculptured image impressively occupies space. This gives it a definite authority and command over the viewer. The image must be seen from all angles to be fully perceived. The viewer must move around it, and each time he moves the image presents a different aspect for contemplation.

Most sculpture is bold, a strong statement of some sort. Because the artist must plan his image from various angles, he must reduce his idea to its simplest elements. If the idea for the image cannot be stripped down to essentials, it will usually not be successful as sculpture.

Translating an idea into such a form has obvious appeal to the maker of images. It also makes certain demands on him. His concept must be valid. It takes time and energy to make a sculpture, and the artist's convictions must be strong enough to sustain his creative drive through the sculpting process.

Making sculpture in wood has several advantages. Wood can be sawed and carved innumerable ways. The cuts may be broad and rough or finely detailed. Because a sculpture has so much surface, the naturally handsome quality of wood is a boon. Wood can also be joined with ease, a particularly important characteristic today. It is extremely difficult for the artist who wants to make a large image to find a large enough piece of his raw material. If working with wood, he can simply glue small pieces together until he has a block the desirable size.

Not all three-dimensional objects are works of art, yet because of their character some are commanding. Some of the examples presented in this chapter were not conceived as art, but they are accepted as such today. The change in attitude indicates a greater appreciation of the skill and energy that went into making the images. Criticized according to a formal set of esthetic principles, a cigar store Indian is not a work of art. Appreciated for its mass and direction in space and its concreteness of idea, it is. This latter view seems preferable, for it gives value to a wider range of human ingenuity and skill.

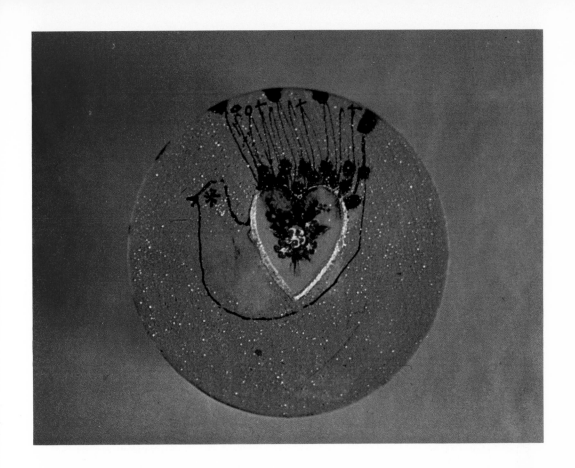

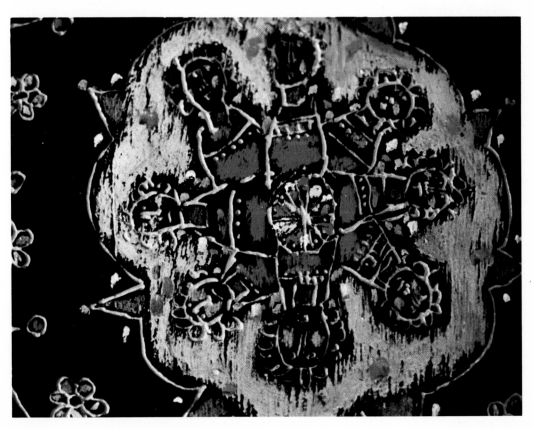

Cigar Store Indian, Delaware, 19th century. (Courtesy of the National Gallery of Art, Index of American Design, Washington.)

Each year two to three hundred cigar store Indians were produced. They were made in large workshops in New York, Chicago, and other centrally located cities, and shipped throughout the country. The typical way of making a cigar store Indian was to carve the body in a white pine log, then attach the arms. Because most carvers were good craftsmen, the joints are hard to detect.

To carve the body, an outline was drawn on the log and the wood was roughly hewn with a chisel and mallet. A good worker could hew about a foot a day. When the figure was roughly revealed, fine carving to finish the shape and add details was done. Then the completely carved and assembled figure was painted. It took about twelve days to make a six-foot Indian.

Cigar Store Indian, Illinois, 19th century. (Courtesy of The National Gallery of Art, Index of American Design, Washington.)

By the mid-nineteenth century, many shops stationed carved figures in front of their doors to advertise their wares. A commercial street must have been a lively sight, with large, brightly painted figures lined up and down the sidewalk. The growth of chain stores and regulations against blocking sidewalks contributed to the demise of this colorful form of advertising.

The reason the Indian is so frequently represented selling cigars is that tobacco was considered the gift of the red man. The history of cigar store Indians is closely related to the history of tobacco. The images were rare before the nineteenth century because tobacco was usually smoked in pipes. When cigar smoking became popular, the making of cigar store figures increased until by 1860 most tobacco shops of any size or repute had their Indians.

Cigar Store Indian, California, 19th century. (Courtesy of The National Gallery of Art, Index of American Design, Washington.)

The tobacconist opened a catalog from any of several cigar store Indian carving shops and chose his model. If he didn't find what he wanted, he had it made to order. Like any business, the cigar store Indian industry had its legends of offbeat orders. One

man from St. Louis supposedly sent a daguerreotype of his mother-in-law and ordered it rendered as a cigar store Indian. The graceful young maiden pictured here was probably not she.

Cigar Store Indian, Michigan, 19th century. (Courtesy of The National Gallery of Art, Index of American Design, Washington.)

The cigar store Indian was designed from reference material and the carver's imagination, mostly the latter. The carver worked from prints in newspapers and magazines, colored lithographs, and, only rarely, from a real Indian model. He elaborated on the buckskin overgarment, leggings, and moccasins supposedly typical of plains Indians by adding feathers, belts of tobacco leaves, beads, garters, and whatever else seemed decorative.

Above, left to right:

Cigar Store Indian, Maryland, 19th century. (Courtesy of the National Gallery of Art, Index of American Design, Washington.)

Many cigar store Indian carvers were master craftsmen; a few were simply glorified carpenters. This image, although awkwardly interpreted, has a certain sturdy boldness which is quite appealing. The face is unusual in that it looks like a portrait of a real person, rather than a standardized version of Indian features.

Cigar Store Indian, New Hampshire, 19th century. (Courtesy of the National Gallery of Art, Index of American Design, Washington.)

Of course the wooden figures became weatherworn from exposure and had to be repainted occasionally. This was sometimes done by traveling artisans who specialized in retouching wooden images but was more often done by a local townsman who was handy with a brush. As each person worked on the Indian, he changed it somewhat to suit his tastes. Thus each factory-made model gradually became

different from its fellows, and the range of representation increased.

Cigar Store Indian, American, ca. 1875. (Courtesy of The New-York Historical Society, New York City.)

The rise of the cigar store Indian parallels the decline of ship carving. Many early craftsmen who had been carvers of ships' figureheads and stern

boards became carvers of Indians. The materials were the same: wood, chisel and mallet, and enamel, so the transition was not difficult. This beautifully finished Indian could be looking either over the plains or over the waves.

Mercury, Cigar Store Figure, Maryland, 19th century. (Courtesy of the National Gallery of Art, Index of American Design, Washington.)

Mercury, messenger of the gods, who moved with tremendous speed, may have been carved to indicate that the tobacconist rapidly filled special orders for tobacco. Figures other than Indians added variety to the breed and individuality to the tobacco shop.

Cigar Store Indian, Maine, 19th century. (Courtesy of the National Gallery of Art, Index of American Design, Washington.)

Among the standard gestures of the cigar store Indian is the hand to the forehead. This has been widely interpreted as gazing over the plains where the buffalo roam, but the gesture was also a salute, a form of greeting. Hello, customer!

Ship's Figurehead, "Columbia," American, 19th century. (Courtesy of the National Gallery of Art, Index of American Design, Washington.)

The different sections of wood used to complete this figure can be clearly seen because they have parted slightly due to weathering and age. The fact that a large block of wood can be easily formed by putting together separate pieces is one of the many reasons wood has been so popular with the carver of images. The pieces in a figurehead were usually put together with dowels, a far more secure joining than that permitted by glue, screws, or nails. Naturally, buffeted by waves, wind, and sea spray, figureheads had to be sturdily pieced together.

Figurehead, "Rosa Isabella," American, 19th century. (Courtesy of the National Gallery of Art, Index of American Design, Washington.)

Representations of some kind have always been popular on ships. The ancient Greeks painted eyes on the prows of their boats to see them safely home, and Americans of the eighteenth and nineteenth centuries carved figureheads. The figures were often women, usually someone connected with the owner or builder of the ship. The figurehead of his ship was regarded by a seaman with affection and superstition. She was kept in top condition, hoping that she would reciprocate by seeing the ship home in good condition.

Dove, probably made in New Hampshire, late 19th century (?). (Courtesy of the National Gallery of Art, Index of American Design, Washington.)

Birds were widely carved in silhouette and in the round as decoys. This bird, although not a decoy (who hunts doves?),

may have been made by a decoy maker for his pleasure and enjoyment. Whoever made it knew birds well. The figure was carved in pine and shellacked.

Figurehead, Rhode Island, early 19th century. (Courtesy of the National Gallery of Art, Index of American Design, Washington.)

A figurehead was carefully planned as part of a ship, and by looking at a detached figurehead one can tell the kind — and date — of the ship for which it was carved. This "bust head" is an early figurehead; it was made to fit a ship with a rounded hull. A little later, full figures standing upright were carved for round-hulled ships. As ships became narrower and their prows more steeply angled, the position of the figureheads changed until they were almost in horizontal poses.

Figurehead, Massachusetts, 19th century. (Courtesy of the National Gallery of Art, Index of American Design, Washington.)

To fully appreciate a figurehead, it must be imagined set in place. This figurehead probably projected quite steeply over the water, judging from the angle of the cut across the base. The figure is spiffily dressed, ready to imposingly greet any foreign port. The high sheen on the image probably results from numerous coats of varnish over glossy enamel.

Grasshopper Weathervane, Massachusetts, 19th century. (Courtesy of the National Gallery of Art, Index of American Design, Washington.)

This grasshopper was carved, then gilded with copper, which caught and reflected the sunlight.

Rooster, American, 19th century. (Collection of the Museum of Early American Folk Art, New York City.)

Animals have always been popular with the makers of images. This carved rooster beautifully shows how the texture of wood can enhance an image. The bird was made from heartwood, or wood at the center of the tree. The center of the tree can be seen on the bird's chest as a small circle from which concentric rings radiate outward. The grain of these rings follows the shape of the body.

Jenny Lind, Rhode Island, ca. 1875. (Courtesy of the National Gallery of Art, Index of American Design, Washington.)

P. T. Barnum's most celebrated venture into the world of culture was the importing of the "Swedish Nightingale," Jenny Lind. She became an overnight smash, partly due to her singing and mostly due to the spectacular promotion by Barnum. Jenny Lind was the subject of drawings, paintings, prints in current magazines, ships' figureheads, and cigar store figures. This wooden image was one of numerous figures on a circus wagon. Whether or not it was a Barnum wagon is unknown.

Carrousel Horse, Rhode Island, 19th century. (Courtesy of the National Gallery of Art, Index of American Design, Washington.)

Most, if not all, carrousel horses were made of wood. It was easy to carve and paint, and comfortable to sit on. (Imagine straddling a nice, cold metal horse.) Holes could be drilled in wood to insert rings or to stuff in a tail made of real horse's hair, as shown here, and decorative nails could be hammered in to embellish the image.

Rocking Horse, Swiss, 1793. (Courtesy of The New-York Historical Society, New York City.)

A clever combination of carving and painting has been used to make this image. The body, head, and handle have been carved in the round, and the legs painted. The separate treatments work successfully as a unit.

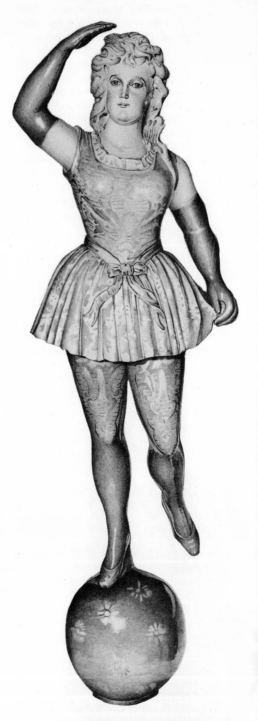

Carrousel Figure: Dancing Girl, American, ca. 1895. (Courtesy of the National Gallery of Art, Index of American Design, Washington.)

Wood can be decorated in almost any style. This pretty, plump beauty of the nineteenth century was marvelously painted. The dress and stockings were particularly skillfully rendered. The figure looks large but is only eighteen inches tall — proof that skill in interpretation creates its own sense of the monumental.

Carrousel goat made by Charles Louff, ca. 1880. (Courtesy of the National Gallery of Art, Index of American Design, Washington.)

A prancing goat must have appealed to a child choosing a place on a carrousel. The image was once a glossy grey, red, orange, brown, green, and black; it is now dull and cracked. This need not have happened, for wood is easy to repaint and keep in good repair.

Liberty by Walter Einsell.

Wood images may express humor, anxiety, love, hate, fear, or any other emotion. Here it is gaily used to interpret the symbol of liberty: crown, torch of truth, and arms opened beside the golden doors.

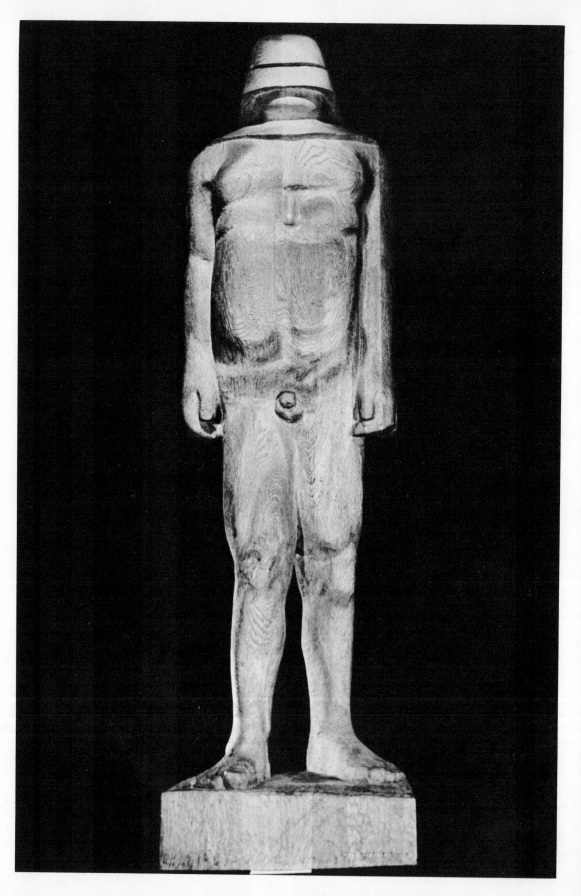

Mother and Child by Henry Moore, 1938. (Courtesy of The Museum of Modern Art, New York City. Acquired through the Lillie P. Bliss Bequest.)

The smooth, flowing relationship between the two parts of this image is implied both by their shapes and their surfaces. The surface is unpainted and sleek, so that the grain shows clearly as a unifying element. The wood is elmwood, a light wood.

←
Warrior by Leonard Baskin. (Photo courtesy of U.S. Plywood Corporation, New York City.)

A print maker whose woodcuts are famous is also a carver of wooden sculptures. Here a powerful figure, identity masked by a helmet, stands immobile, yet somehow threatening. The wood is unpainted walnut.

Socrates by Constantin Brancusi, 1923. (Courtesy of The Museum of Modern Art, New York City, Mrs. Simon Guggenheim Fund.)

The knotty questions posed by Socrates and the bold discussion encouraged by him have been abstracted into a handsome wooden image.

Tilted Construction by Gabriel Kohn, 1959. (Courtesy of The Museum of Modern Art, New York City, Philip C. Johnson Fund.)

Pieces of wood have been laminated to form a solid and imposing image. Each section has been planned so that the grain runs in different directions.

Hollow Form (*Penwith*) by Barbara Hepworth. (Courtesy of The Museum of Modern Art, New York City, gift of Dr. and Mrs. Arthur Lejwa.)

The natural color of wood may be completely retained, or parts of an image colored to bring certain areas into focus. Here stain has been used. Stain does not simply rest on the surface of the wood, it is absorbed by it. Subtle gradations and texture can be achieved by using wood that stains unevenly, as does the lagoswood used to create this sculpture.

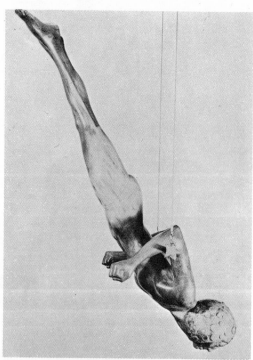

The Star by Sidney Simon. (Photo courtesy of U.S. Plywood Corporation, New York City.)

Sculpture may be used anywhere, standing on the floor, projecting from a wall or the prow of a ship, or hanging from the ceiling. Where it is to be displayed affects its design. Viewed from below, this sculpture conveys the startling impression of looming through space.

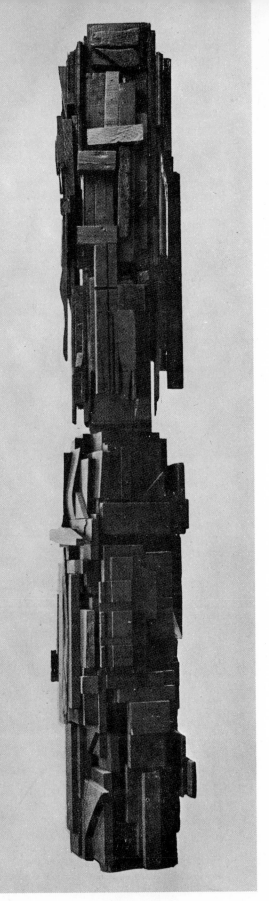

Sky Column I by Louise Nevelson. (Photo courtesy of U.S. Plywood Corporation, New York City.)

Wood is so common in buildings that its use architecturally for an image is natural. This free-standing image is composed of numerous pieces of planks, all painted in a flat dark color. The eye is moved over the image in response to the darks and not-so-darks created by the various planes in the image.

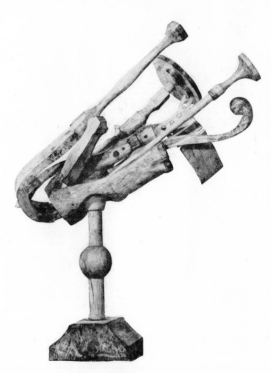

Lafcadio by John Anderson. (Photo courtesy of U.S. Plywood Corporation, New York City.)

This dynamic image incorporates both natural wood and lumber. In the center appears to be a tree stump stripped of its bark. The whole image bursts outward and upward, yet it is heavily centered, structurally and conceptually.

Virgin and Child, French (School of Auvergne), 12th century. (Courtesy of The Metropolitan Museum of Art, New York City, Gift of J. Pierpont Morgan, 1916.)

The artist makes a choice: he can either define the form or decorate it. The maker of this wooden image abstracted the drapery on the figure to form a bold, static pattern. But notice in the Madonna how the folds swirl downward on the upper part of her body and upward on her legs. By this device the artist has focused the viewer on the child far more effectively than if he had chosen to carve the folds realistically.

Christ Child, Spanish, 17th century. (Collection of Carol Roemer Kaechele, Topanga, California.)

Because wooden images were easy to produce in quantity, many were brought to Mexico from Spain. This small figure was originally part of a large image, perhaps a manger scene or Holy Family group. The wood was colored with some kind of glossy paint, and the eyes, which are set in the wood, are polished stone.

St. Barbara (?), Italian, 18th century.

The bust and forearms in this statue were finely carved, covered with gesso, and polychromed. These are the only original parts of the statue. The original body and legs were made of cloth and stuffed, so that the figure could be arranged in various poses. These stuffed parts have long since deteriorated, so the remaining pieces have been nailed onto a wooden armature for preservation. The armature has been so cleverly made that the assembled pieces look like a complete statue.

Christ (detail), Mexican, 18th century.

The Mexicans copied Spanish religious art for several years, but then gradually replaced it with a style of their own. This detail is a good example of what happens when two worlds meet. Before the arrival of Spanish Catholicism, the Mexicans adhered to a pantheon of vengeful, bloodthirsty native gods and made appropriate images of them. Even after their conversion, they continued this kind of representation, producing this extremely bloody and painful interpretation of Christ crucified. This concept of the crucifixion is probably closer to the truth than the sophisticated, cleaned up images of western Europe.

The glass eyes in this figure are framed by real eye lashes, and the hair is real human hair. The crown of thorns is metal, and so sharp that it cuts if not handled carefully. The face was roughly carved and gesso used to create a smooth surface. The beard was built up with gesso, not carved in wood.

Crucifix from the Church of the Convent of Santa Clara, Province of Leon, Spain, 12th century. (Courtesy of The Metropolitan Museum of Art, New York City, The Cloisters Collection Samuel D. Lee Fund, 1935.)

This religious image has a strangely detached expression which can be interpreted in numerous ways, depending on what the viewer brings to the image. Because this figure is three-dimensional, occupying space in the same way the viewer is, the confrontation between image and viewer is more forceful than if the crucifix had been painted on a flat surface.

ASSEMBLED IMAGES

There are several advantages in putting together an image from separate pieces. Often it is just plain practical to shape each piece individually and then assemble the whole. Sometimes the image has details or features, such as movable joints, which would be impossible to handle otherwise. At other times, when certain areas of the image are to receive special treatment in terms of texture, delicacy, or detail, it would be downright wasteful not to capitalize on wood's unique quality of being able to be cut apart and fastened together again with ease. The special treatment can be worked out with greater freedom in separate pieces than if the area remains part of the entire image.

Assembling images also permits the image maker to incorporate a wide range of objects in his image. Metals, plastics, fabrics, and other natural and man-made materials can be used. They may be raw materials or ready-made objects.

The freedom permitted by assembling images encourages imaginative use of the materials. The possible reasons for assembling an image have been summarized in this chapter in three sections: A whole divided into parts, images with movable parts, and assemblage.

A Whole Divided Into Parts

In this approach the image maker carefully plans the entire image, often in great detail, and then divides it into parts. He knows exactly what he wants and decides that working up each piece separately is better than trying to work on a whole block.

Often it is difficult to get at certain areas of a block with woodworking tools. Carving and incising tools require space in which to be maneuvered. The artist working in wood has a choice: he may either commit himself to working on an entire block, knowing he probably will have to endure the discomfort of physical contortions to get at certain areas, or he can remove a section and work on it with ease. A separate piece can be turned and worked with a great deal of freedom, then replaced and the joint carefully hidden from all but the most discerning eye.

The image maker may want to use different kinds of wood in his image. Woods come in a wide variety of color, texture, and grain. He may decide to assemble different kinds for visual effects. Or, he may decide to carve certain areas in great detail and leave others relatively plain.

Fine woods for carving are expensive. The artist may buy these woods only for the areas to be carved and use other woods for the plainer areas.

There is also the question of conserving time, energy, and materials. Why carve away a large chunk of wood to get, say, a simple detail bridging two separate areas? The areas can be carved, and the object bridging them developed in a small segment of wood and then set in.

The reasons for dividing a whole into separate parts are as numerous as the images developed this way. As you examine the following images, the reasons for working them or parts of them in separate pieces will be clear.

Blocks by Milton Glaser.

A block has six faces, and each block in this group bears six different designs. By simply turning one block, the assembled image changes. Literally, over a million different images can be formed with this set.

Model of a Slaughter House, from the Tomb of Mehenktre, Thebes, Egypt, XI Dynasty. (Courtesy of The Metropolitan Museum of Art, New York City, Museum Excavations, 1919-1920, Rogers Fund supplemented by contribution of Edward S. Harkness, 1920.)

Here is a model of a slaughter house, insurance that the afterworld would contain a source of steaks and roasts.

St. Martin and the Beggar, Mexican, 20th century.

It is often easier to carve each piece of an image separately and then assemble the pieces. Here various parts of the same image are shown disassembled and assembled. The method of joining the pieces together is by using dowels. One part bears the dowel, and another has a hole to receive it.

Shawabti Figures of Princess Entiu-ny, from the Tomb of Queen Meryet-Amun, Deir el Bahri, Thebes, Egypt, XXI Dynasty, ca. 1025 B.C. (Courtesy of The Metropolitan Museum of Art, New York City, Museum Excavations, 1928-1929), Rogers Fund, 1930.)

As part of their burial equipment, members of the royal family had images carved to represent those people they might need in the afterworld.

Model of a Cattle Stable, from the Tomb of Meket-Re, Egyptian, XI Dynasty, ca. 2000 B.C. (Courtesy of The Metropolitan Museum of Art, New York City, Museum Excavations, 1919-1920, Rogers Fund supplemented by contribution of Edward S. Harkness.)

The image tells a lot about how cows were cared for in ancient Egypt, and illustrates how wooden images have played a role in capturing and recording moments in history.

Models: Cow and Calf, from Meir, Egyptian, XII Dynasty. (Courtesy of The Metropolitan Museum of Art, New York City, Rogers Fund, 1911.)

These charming animals were made separately and assembled on a plank. They are fixed in place because their legs fit into holes drilled in the plank. When planning to assemble an image this way, the artist must keep in mind that that part of the figure going into the hole will be lost from the viewer's sight. Therefore, in this case, the artist made the legs longer than he would have if the animals were just to be glued on the plank.

Toy Wooden Cannon, American, ca. 1845. (Courtesy of The New-York Historical Society, New York City.)

The reasons for planning this image as separate parts are obvious. Trying to carve a round cannon barrel still attached to a block is much more difficult than shaping a separate piece of wood or just using a round stick. Also, to move, the wheels cannot be attached. They must be separate, so why not carve them separately?

Fishing and Fowling Skiff: Harpooning Fish, from the Tomb of Meket-Re, Egyptian, XI Dynasty, ca. 2000 B.C. (Courtesy of The Metropolitan Museum of Art, New York City, Museum Excavations, 1919-1920, Rogers Fund, supplemented by contribution of Edward S. Harkness.)

Not only has each figure in this image been carved separately, but parts of each figure have been also worked individually. The paddles, oars, and harpoons have been inserted into the hands after the person and tool were completely carved. The image was probably gessoed and painted after the parts had been assembled. The gesso and paint help bind them in place.

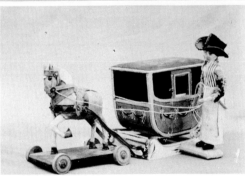

Toy Sled, Dutch, 18th century. Courtesy of The Metropolitan Museum of Art, New York City, Bequest of Mrs. Maria P. James, 1911.)

Because wood is so easily combined with other materials, it is frequently ornamented with them or put together with them. Here the horse is attached to the sled with leather thongs, and the coachman to the horse with cord. In this case, such tenuous attachments were practical. The child who owned the toy could take it apart easily to play with the separate pieces, and then reassemble them when his imagination called for it.

Adam and Eve and the Tree of Life by José Dolores Lopez, ca. 1930. (Courtesy of The Museum of Modern Art, New York City, Gift of Mrs. Meredith Hare.)

Adam and Eve have been assembled in the classic manner; that is, the separate parts of their bodies have been glued together. However, the apples and leaves have been attached in a rather unique way. One end of a length of stiff wire was pushed into an apple and the other end forced into the tree. No drilling of holes was necessary, thanks to the softness of the wood, cottonwood.

73

Statuette: Horse and Rider, Egyptian, early XVIII Dynasty. (Courtesy of The Metropolitan Museum of Art, New York City, Rogers Fund, 1915.)

Here the legs and arms of the rider and the rider himself were carved before the rider was put on the horse. But notice how closely the rider fits on the horse. When working this way, the carver must periodically put the unfinished pieces together to see that they fit snugly.

The Royal Architect, Ka-pu-nesut, Sakkara, Egypt, V-VI Dynasty. (Courtesy of The Metropolitan Museum of Art, New York City, Rogers Fund, 1926.)

The arms were joined to the body with dowels. The statue was then covered with gesso, which hid the seams, and painted. Most of the gesso and paint have worn off.

Mask of Christ, Mexican, 18th century. (Courtesy of Lloyd E. Kaechele, Palo Alto, California.)

The teeth, which can barely be seen in this photograph, were set in with glue. Incidentally, they are real human teeth.

Father Time, American, 19th century. (Courtesy of the Museum of Early American Folk Arts, New York City.)

The places where this figure has been assembled can be clearly seen: the ankles, the arms, and the wings.

Noah's Ark, American, late 19th century. (Courtesy of The New-York Historical Society, New York City.)

An image composed of separate parts does not have to be structurally linked to be complete. Noah's ark and its animals are an example. By itself, the ark is incomplete, somehow barren. With animals placed in any position around it, the idea is complete.

Crucifix by Bill Greer.

This image has been made from many separate parts. The halo, cross, leaves, and seraphim were separate pieces which have been glued together. They were carved separately because it was just plain easier. The assembled image was stained and waxed with shoe polish.

Roller Coaster by William Accorsi.

This roller coaster is the quintessence of why one might assemble an image. It is huge, fifteen feet long and twelve feet wide. The entire thing was carefully planned, and the separate sections built with dowels. The uphill sections have motorized pulleys between the tracks to catch the cars and bring them to the top, just as in a real roller coaster.

Images with Movable Parts

Wood comes from a living thing, and motion is one of the characteristics of life. Wood is therefore, conceptually and technically, the ideal material for images with movable parts.

The ease of working in wood contributes to the ultimate success of a movable image. Joints may be fashioned by sawing and carving. The pieces forming the joint may be hinged with numerous materials. They can be drilled to insert dowels or nuts and bolts which serve as metal axles. A joint can simply turn on a nail. Wood also moves against wood easily, requiring little or no treatment other than shaping to make motion possible.

Tic-Tac-Toe.

The ladies against the gentlemen in this sporting version of an old game. The pieces for the game were made by gluing old pictures on flat squares of wood. On the top edge of each piece is a large eyelet that fits onto the cuphooks in the board.

Merry-Go-Round, India, 20th century. (Courtesy of Scarabaeus, Ltd., New York City.)

A merry-go-round from India is shown disassembled (bottom of page) and assembled. The top, propellor-like wheel rotates on the point of the pole.

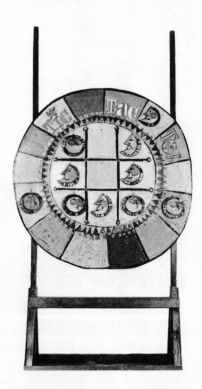

Tic-Tac-Toe, A Variation.

Another version of the same game, in which the day people play the night people. The round board was cut from plywood and colored with water-base paint and oil crayons. Then it was shellacked to protect it. If you look closely, you can see where screws were used to attach the board to its stand.

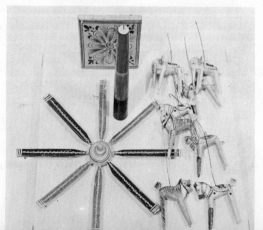

Wheels of Fortune by Karen Eisen.

These two images (left and right) were done on composition board, which is softer and more absorbent than plywood. The board is made of different kinds of wood chips pressed together. The various chips absorb paint differently, giving the surface an irregular, soft impression similar to that of frescos.

There are three movable wheels in each image. Each wheel spins independently. Those on the left and right in each image are mounted on the surface of the image. They turn on small metal axles. The face in the triangle above the head of the man (or woman) is painted on the third wheel. This wheel is mounted on the back and is turned by spinning that part of the wheel which can barely be seen at the bottom of the image. Incidentally, the words on the wheels were made with pressure-sensitive letters, which are available at art supply stores. They were shellacked to prevent their being rubbed off.

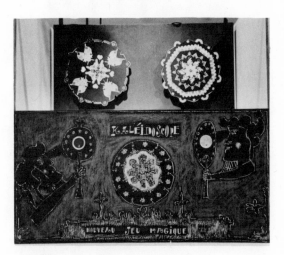

The Kaleidoscope.

Two store-bought kaleidoscopes were mounted in the front board. These are focused on the two wheels on the back board, which are motorized and revolve slowly. The repetitive decoration on each wheel was made by making several photostats of an interesting motif and arranging the photostats on the wheel. Hand-drawn motifs, magazine cutouts, and stenciled designs could also have been used. The kaleidoscopes are a special kind; they do not contain bits of paper or whatever. They contain lenses that fragment and distort whatever they are focused on.

The Oracle.

This image was also made on composition board. It was colored with Dr. Martin's dyes and oil crayons. The one flaw of composition board is that it can be chipped around the edges very readily. This is not a particularly important consideration unless the image is to be moved around a lot or handled roughly.

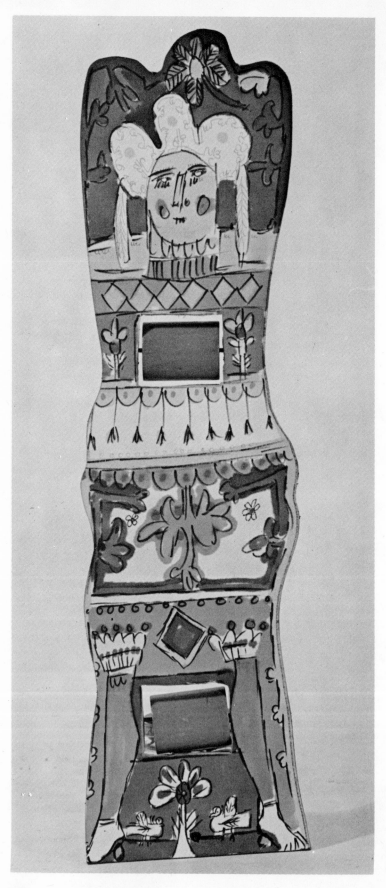

Pull Toy.

A piece of wood was cut, then colored with magic markers. A short length of dowel was fitted into holes cut in the wood. Short pieces of straight wire cut from coat hangers were inserted through the dowels, and the wire fastened to the back of the board with staples.

Whirligigs and Weathervanes, American, 19th century. (Collection of Joseph B. Martinson. Photo courtesy of the Museum of Early American Folk Arts, New York City.)

All these figures move in the wind. Most of the pieces move on simple axles made with nails, bolts, or metal rods. To move easily, a joint must be smooth, and it is simple to carve or sand wood until the joint is perfect. In the photograph, count the variety of forms that can be made to move around a simple joint.

Puppets

Almost anything can be used to hinge two pieces so that they move. Here cord joins arms to bodies, feet to legs. These amusing puppets were cut with a scissors from sheets of balsa wood, which can be easily punched with a nail to make holes for the string.

83

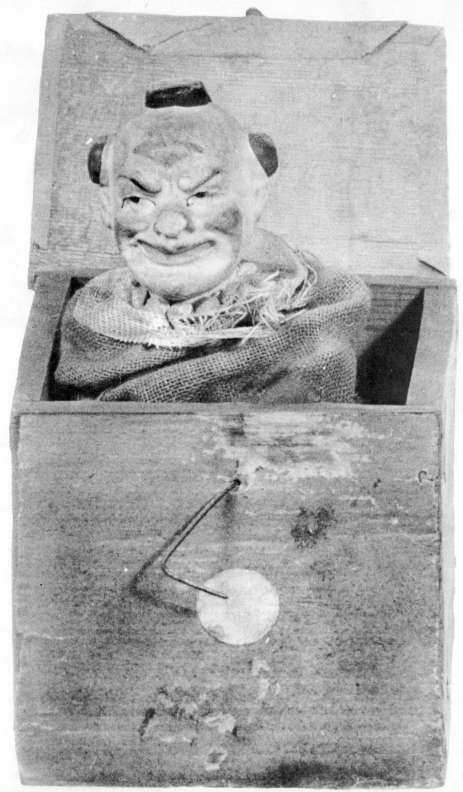

Jack-in-the-Box, American, early 19th century. (Courtesy of The New-York Historical Society, New York City.)

A large spring makes the jack jump up when the lid is raised. One end of the spring is nailed to the bottom of the box, and the other fastened to the base of the head. The spring is concealed by a loose burlap garment.

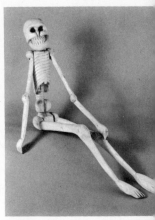

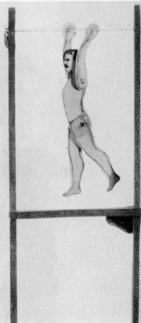

Top Row, left to right:
Whirligig, American, late 19th century. (Courtesy of the National Gallery of Art, Index of American Design, Washington.)

How can you keep normal, boisterous children calm on the Sabbath? The Pennsylvania Dutch had an answer, the whirligig. These toys were invented to quietly entertain the children of this strict people.

Jack-in-the-Box, American, early 19th century. (Courtesy of The New-York Historical Society, New York City.)

Oops. Look who's here! Jack jumped up via the spring concealed by his striped robe.

Whirligig, Pennsylvania, late 19th century. (Courtesy of the National Gallery of Art, Index of American Design, Washington.)

Both the figure and the arms revolve in this whirligig. The image was carved in pine and painted with oil colors.

Skeleton, from Oaxaca, Mexico, ca. 1960. (Courtesy of Mr. and Mrs. J. T. Ungerer.)

The arms and legs of this skeleton move on the most simple of all possible axles — the nail.

Bottom Row, left to right:
Toy Accordion, German, 19th century.
Max and Morris, the original Katzenjammer kids, are seen in this image in a very untypical pose: they are up to no mischief.

Uncle Sam and John Bull, American, 19th century.

Paper cutouts were mounted on wood. The arms move on brads, similar to the kind you buy in a stationery store.

The Acrobat, American, ca. 1876. (Courtesy of The New-York Historical Society, New York City.)

The two upright sticks pivot on small bolts attached to the crossbar. As the uprights are pulled apart at the bottom, their tops come close together, letting the figure on his string relax. The sudden tension caused by quickly pulling the uprights parallel makes the acrobat swing upward and whirl.

The Spirit of '76 by William Accorsi.

The amount of ingenuity and work that went into this image is staggering. The figures in front, whose joints should be closely examined, are attached to a crossbar. This crossbar, in turn, is attached to a long stick that extends back to the castle. Within the castle a small electric motor turns a wheel that makes the stick go up and down, dropping the figures in front onto the plank. The impact makes them tap their feet and the spring arms jiggle, beating the drum, waving the flag, and tooting the horn. Meanwhile, back at the castle, a music box, also electrically run, is playing *Yankee Doodle*.

Assemblage

Art is a reflection of its time, and the artist draws upon the materials typical of his time to mirror it. One of the most typical materials of our time is junk, the last phase of once practical objects.

Never before has there been so much junk. Its omnipresence compels contemplation of it. One person may look at it symbolically as the refuse of person or persons unknown; another may completely divorce it emotionally and intellectually from its previous use and see it in terms of shapes, textures, and lines. Both can use it to assemble a work of art.

There are two ways of working with junk. In one, the artist has an image in mind and finds discarded objects to develop it. In the other approach, which is quite common today, an artist collects bits and pieces of junk and begins to experiment with them. The image emerges as he experiments.

The following examples show what can be done with junk and other ready-made objects. Such images are sometimes called Found Art, for their components already existed, waiting to be appreciated, evaluated, and incorporated into a work of art. Images so constructed are also called assemblages, a word describing not the objects but how they were used. They were assembled.

For Married Women, For Single Girls

A found object may be completely divorced from its previous context, or retain its function and be altered only in some slight way. Here an old "drop a penny in the slot . . ." machine has been decorated by replacing its original face with a wooden plaque and painting it in gay colors. The original cards were replaced with fortune cards designed by the maker of the wooden image. And inflation has not set in; a penny still buys the message.

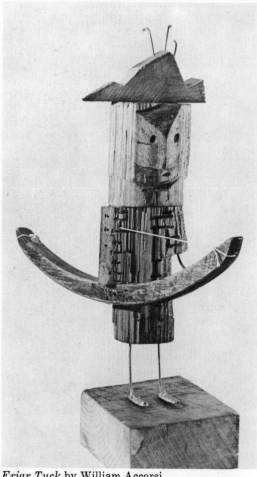

Friar Tuck by William Accorsi.

Robin Hood's valiant companion has been assembled from materials typical of his legendary home, the forest. The bow is the only modern addition; it is a coat hanger.

The Masked Intruder by William Accorsi.

Door pulls off chests of drawers, nails, costume jewelry, and scraps of wood were assembled to form this romantic (look at the mask) image. In the hands of the artist, junk can be elevated to art.

Brushbird by Tomi Ungerer. (Courtesy of Miriam Ungerer.)

The odd bits of flotsam and jetsam used in this image are junk retrieved from a trash can and a vacant lot. The body of the bird is made of a slice of wood so weathered that its grain is quite distinct. The battered brush gives the bird a somewhat ruffled look, as if he were saying, "What's this about junk in art?"

Rocking Horse by William Accorsi.

An assembled image can be practical. This charming hobby horse is made of an unpainted stool mounted on barrel staves, and two kinds of brushes.

Poem-Object by Andre Breton, 1941. (Courtesy of The Museum of Modern Art, New York City, The Kay Sage Tanguy Bequest.)

A carved wood bust of a man, an oil lantern, a framed photograph, toy boxing gloves, and black paper were mounted on a drawing board to make this provocative wooden image.

Two Children are Threatened by a Nightingale by Max Ernst, 1924. (Courtesy of The Museum of Modern Art, New York City.)

This is a strange combination of painting and construction. The gate and post are made of wood, as is part of the shed, which projects from the painting. The heavy wooden frame closes in on the scene, increasing the nightmarish feeling of it.

Moon by Robert Indiana, 1960. (Courtesy of The Museum of Modern Art, New York City, Philip C. Johnson Fund.)

A wooden beam serves as a central trunk for this upright image. The wheels, which are iron, make the image look somewhat like a rearing locomotive — potentially powerful, but helpless in this position. The moons were done with white paint.

The Family by Marisol (Marisol Escobar), 1962. (Courtesy of The Museum of Modern Art, New York City, Advisory Committee Fund.)

Marisol, the master of bizarre assemblages, has combined painting, drawing, sculpting, and junk to give us this capsule statement about matriarchy.

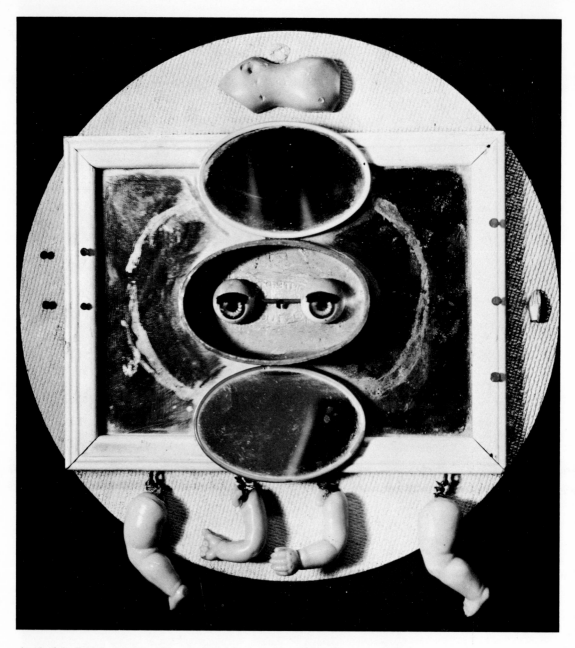

Anybody's Self Portrait by George Cohen. (Courtesy of The Museum of Modern Art, New York City, Larry Aldrich Foundation Fund.)

The disjointed individual, out of contact with himself and with others, is brilliantly captured through assemblage. The basic ingredients are a framed square mirror mounted on painted masonite. On top were added two oval mirrors, a plastic doll's torso, painted doll's eyes with fiber lashes in an anchovy tin can, etc., etc. Anything is raw material for an assemblage, and startling messages can be stated with found objects.

PROJECTS AND PROBLEMS

This chapter contains projects for making wooden images. The projects are designed for individuals as well as for teachers who wish to stimulate and capture the imagination of their students.

The material has been divided into four parts: Basic Considerations, Simple Projects, Intermediate Projects, and Advanced Projects. The projects in each section contain the germ of an idea and advice on solving any problems that might arise in designing or working out the image in wood.

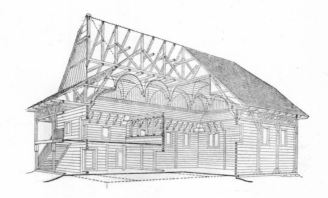

Basic Considerations

The essence of being able to work easily and creatively in wood lies in understanding its qualities as a material. The following projects are designed to help you or, if you are a teacher, your students explore some of the characteristics that make wood so exciting to work with.

Project 1. Learning to appreciate wood.

This project is intended to stimulate the study of wood in nature, art, and architecture. The idea is to learn something about wood in its natural state and how its basic features can be altered or exploited to suit some particular function.

First look at wood in its natural state, in trees, bushes and woody stemmed plants. Notice its tremendous variety in shape, size and color. Bark in some species is smooth and thin. In other species it is rough with distinct swirls, angles, and planes. Gather chunks of wood, bark, forked branches, and chips for later study and experimentation.

Explore the seashore and the banks of lakes and streams for wood tossed up by waves or lying partially submerged. Notice how water has affected them. Some water-worn specimens are extremely handsome. When they dry out, notice how they have changed in character. You may want to try weathering wood by submersion, or to imitate some of the effects of wet wood.

Look at the wood in various buildings. The wood in old buildings is frequently worn into interesting shapes and textures. Examine how artisans of yesteryear put wood together for maximum support and beauty. You may learn some tricks that are helpful in constructing wooden images. Compare the appearance of painted and unpainted buildings of the same age. Does the comparison suggest anything you might want to consider if your wooden image is planned for outdoor display?

Also look around for loose finished wood and collect it for later use. Search the scrap piles around building sites, lumber yards, and junk yards. Compare the way these pieces have been cut out. How does the way in which they were cut affect their appearance? How does the type of cut affect the grain? How can you use these observations?

94

Project 2. Intimations from wood.

Each piece of wood is different. Even two pieces of wood from the same tree, cut the same size, vary in grain, warp, and color. Examine the pieces of wood you have collected and look for ideas in the wood itself. This is somewhat like looking at a cloud and seeing shapes in it. Perhaps a knothole suggests an eye or a balloon. Perhaps a swirl in the grain looks like a horse's mane, or a wave. Develop what the wood suggests by painting, drawing, or sawing the rest of the image.

A whole chunk of wood may look like something. For example, a forked branch may resemble a body with legs. By adding other found objects as feet, hands, and head, the image can be completed.

When you consider that each piece of wood may suggest numerous images, you can see that the possibilities in this project are endless.

Painted Decor, American, late 18th century. (Courtesy of The Cooper Union Museum, New York City.)

Project 3. Coloring wood.

In coloring wood you are limited only by the number and kinds of coloring agents available and your imagination. Try anything that comes to hand — a child's watercolors, old lipsticks, house paints, crayons, commercial stains, artist's oils. Have fun with this.,Try mashing a fresh blackberry between two pieces of plank. The resulting Rorschach-like stain may be a satisfying design as is, or it may be completed by adding details with other kinds of paints and stains.

Goony Bird by Tomi Ungerer. (Photo courtesy of D'Arcy Galleries, New York City.)

Learn the differences in surface and sheen among the various coloring agents. Which will give you fine lines and permit extensive detailing? Which dry practically on contact, and which take days to dry? Can you mix colors directly on the wood? What happens when you apply wax crayons and then paint over them with water-base paints?

What happens when you wet wood with water and then apply water-base paints? Oil-base paints? How does applying artist's oils over wood soaked with paint thinner look? Look at your various efforts a few weeks later. Have the original effects changed?

Try using different applicators. A fine-pointed pen or brush gives a different effect than a blunt stick dipped in paint. When can you use spray guns or cloth pads to make coloring easier?

These are questions you should answer yourself. By simply experimenting without any projects in mind you may pick up some techniques that will add immeasurably to the success of a planned image.

William Accorsi

Figurehead from "Henrietta Francis," a ship built in Massachusetts in 1883. (Courtesy of the National Gallery of Art, Index of American Design, Washington.)

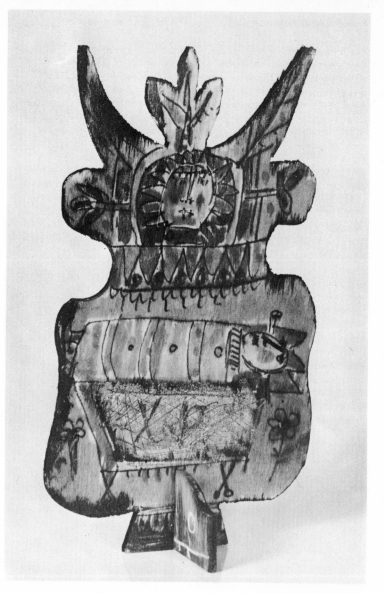

Project 4. Scratching wood.

Most wood is soft enough to be easily scratched with a sharp nail. Try it. Cross-hatch, or angle all scratches in the same direction. Draw up and down and around. Try any line you

would attempt with a pencil. Then see how much surface texture you can create with the nail by scratching along interesting natural patterns in the grain. Scratch the wood before you paint it and scratch it after you paint it. How do you like the different effects? What can you do with them?

What other tools can you find around the house which will

make interesting lines? The kind of rowel used in marking the tops of pies can be used for dotted lines on wood. Pizza-cutters can be run across wood for a continuous fine line. When you have exhausted the potential tools around the house, explore your local hardware and art supply stores for additional tools.

Project 5. Carving wood.

When you see how scratching enhances the surface of the wood, you will want to experiment with other ways of cutting patterns in wood. Begin with a simple design problem: the creation of an over-all pattern by carving shallow cuts

in a flat plank. Your design may be based on natural patterns in the wood, or be independent of these patterns. Using any sharp knife, carefully cut out slivers and chips. Notice how the angle of the cut affects the shape left in the board. A great deal of variety in shape can be achieved simply by varying the carving angle.

Simple design-and-cut projects teach basic design considerations, such as the effect of dark and light areas on a surface, and technical skills, including short cuts in wood working. After experimenting with a few different woods, you will find that some kinds are easier to carve than others. Also, the grain may make carving difficult, which, of course, influences how intricate the design can be. In most woods, the shallower the cut, the easier it is to remove the sliver or chip.

When you have experimented with designing over-all patterns on a flat plank, try modeling with the knife. Cut around the edges of a plank to soften and enhance the borders. Take cubes of wood or logs or forked branches and carve them. A little practice will indicate the tools and woods best suited for carving purposes.

Reed Pipe, American Indian (Northwest Coast). (Courtesy of The Metropolitan Museum of Art, New York City, the Crosby Brown Collection of Musical Instruments, 1889.)

Wheat, Rhode Island, 19th century. (Courtesy of the National Gallery of Art, Index of American Design, Washington.)

Mangle board, Dutch, 18th century. (Courtesy of The Metropolitan Museum of Art, New York City, Rogers Fund, 1911.)

Cookie Mold, Missouri, 19th century. (Courtesy of the National Gallery of Art, Index of American Design, Washington.)

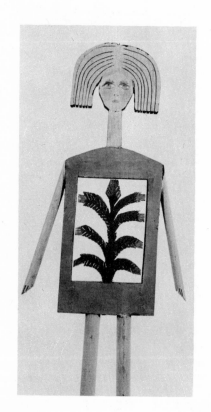

Project 6. Cutting wood.

Because wood is easy to cut, it offers a wealth of design possibilities. It permits wood to become an integral part of the image, rather than just a support for other art materials.

Hose Holder — Fire Company Insignia, Philadelphia, ca. 1820. (Courtesy of the National Gallery of Art, Index of American Design, Washington.)

To appreciate what can be done using only a saw and a plank, start with a simple flat square of wood. At this point don't remove pieces of the square, just use the saw to make lines in the plank that break up its austere surface. Try some long and short parallel cuts, some at different angles, some closer together, others far apart. Create an almost lacy pattern with your flat square.

Then take another square plank. You may change the shape of this one by removing sections from the edges and interior. Cuts along the edges should be easy, and you will find a narrow bladed saw good for circular cuts. (For details on what kind of saws are appropriate for particular cuts, see Tools and Materials, p.9). Try a variety of cut shapes around the periphery.

Cuts in the interior of the plank may pose problems. Small round holes are easy; simply use a drill. Large, irregularly shaped cuts may be much more difficult. For information on how to start and cut these shapes, see Tools and Materials, p.8 . Try at least a few kinds of interior cuts. No matter how limited you are by the available tools or your technical skill, making interior cuts is an excellent means of focusing attention in the center of the image.

Project 7. Nails and decoration.

Nails are not only functional, they can also be used as decoration. Carpenter's nails come in several sizes, textures, and, surprisingly, colors. Roofing nails are short, squat, rough-textured, and dull grey, and have very large heads. Finishing nails are slender, shiny silver in color, and have almost no head. Some nails, like carpet tacks, are a purplish black; others are bronze. And these nails are only carpenter's nails. There are others! Upholsterers use nails with decorated heads. There are flower-shaped heads, round heads, and heads bearing many kinds of embossed motifs. They are red, green, orange, blue, brown, brass, silver, and other colors. Since nails come in such variety and are made for use with wood, why not use them in designing a wooden image?

Take a flat board and a variety of nails. These nails are to be hammered into the wood to form a design. Some may be hammered in up to the head, others just slightly tapped in. You can create a design with the nails that has relief as well as surface interest, and this effect can be incorporated in the design of numerous wooden images.

Project 8. Putting wood together.

Return to your collection of found and scrap wood and pick up any two pieces. Arrange them together. Put one on top of the other; abut them; place them at angles in different planes.

Just play around until you get something that pleases you, then

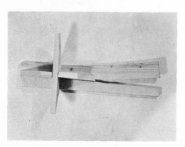

analyze why. Is it the greater surface, and therefore greater visual involvement, permitted by using more than one piece of wood? Is it the resulting direction or indication of space? Is it the naturally created planes and areas of light and dark? Is it all of these? Then put your favorite combination together with nails or glue and keep it for future study.

Now, randomly select three pieces and try the same thing. Now four, and so on. This project moves you conceptually into thinking about free-standing sculpture. The ease of working with wood indicates why wood is a favorite of sculptors.

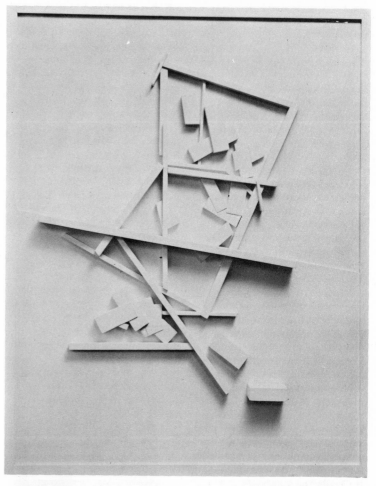

White Anxiety by Gertrude Greene. (Courtesy of The Museum of Modern Art, New York City, Gift of Balcomb Greene.)

Project 9. Antiquing surfaces.

Aged surfaces are often quite handsome and can add to the impact of an image designed to suggest things or ideas antique. The techniques of antiquing are all based on the fact that old things are generally weathered, worn, and torn, and these features are fairly easy to recreate artificially.

A piece of wood can be punched with a nail or an awl to make "wormholes" and scratched with the same implements to imitate the wear and tear of use. The trick in faking these characteristics is to remember that they were originally made haphazardly. Evenly spaced scratches and punctures look deliberate and therefore phony. One artist we know lets his children use the planks intended for his "antique" wooden images as dart boards. The resulting punctures, nicks, and scrapes are quite naturalistic.

Have you ever wondered how factory fresh, genuine imitation Spanish Colonial and Provincial furniture gets that antique look? There are artisans who specialize in "distressing" it. To imitate the bumps, punctures, and chips typical of old furniture, they beat new furniture with chains. This kind of antiquing could be quite effective on a wooden image, but it is not recommended for children or awkward adults. However, the careful adult should be able to distress his image with ease, using inexpensive chains from a hardware store.

Paint is more difficult to antique than wood. Old paint is frequently chipped or has fine cracks. Cracked paint may be effected by applying paint over a base that dries more slowly than the paint or contracts more than the paint while drying. An artist's handbook on materials is a good source for learning which paints and bases to use. You will usually find the topic listed under flaws in painting techniques.

However, a flaw in a painting may be an asset in a wooden image.

Today you can buy sets of paints chemically composed to give an antique look. These are fairly easy to use, if you follow directions, and the finished surface looks authentically antique.

Madonna, New Mexico, 19th century. (Courtesy of the National Gallery of Art, Index of American Design, Washington.)

Toy Horse, American, 19th century. (Courtesy of the National Gallery of Art, Index of American Design, Washington.)

Paul Davis

William Accorsi

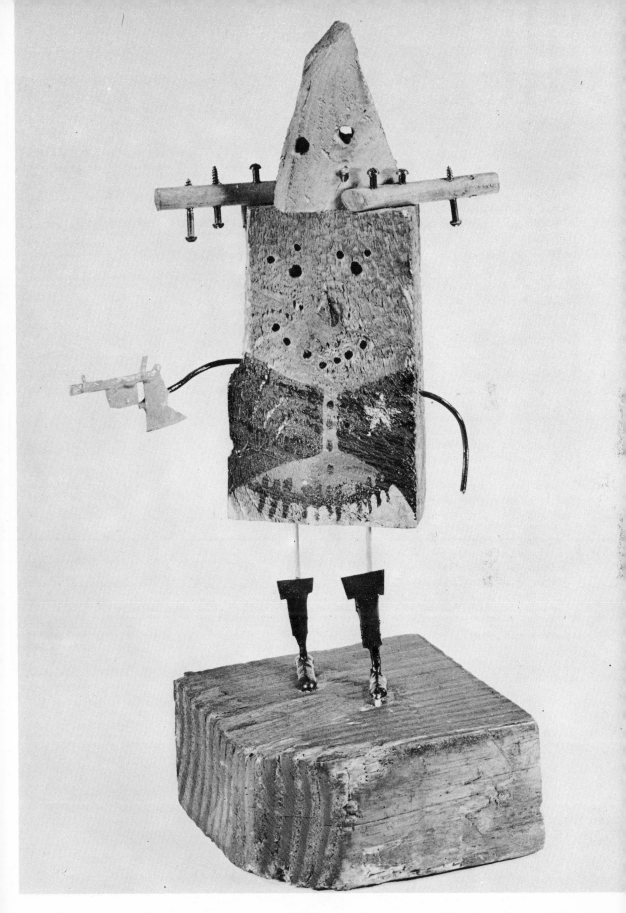

Simple Projects

These projects require very little skill in handling tools and materials. Some of them may be done with precut wood, and others require only the simplest shaping. Because they are easy and quick to do, they are particularly suitable for children and adults who have never before made any kind of image in wood. Although the ideas are simple, there is room for a great deal of imagination in carrying them out.

Project 10. Stick figures.

Any wooden object can be used to develop a wooden image. Here is a project that is an exercise in imagination. Start with the sticks used for stirring paint which are usually donated free by hardware stores and paint supply dealers. How can you develop an image on a long, narrow, flat piece of wood? Try anything: sawing and incising the wood; coloring it with inks and paints; gluing plain pieces of colored paper and figurative cutouts on it; stapling on it or inserting in it bells, flowers, trinkets, or other small three-dimensional objects.

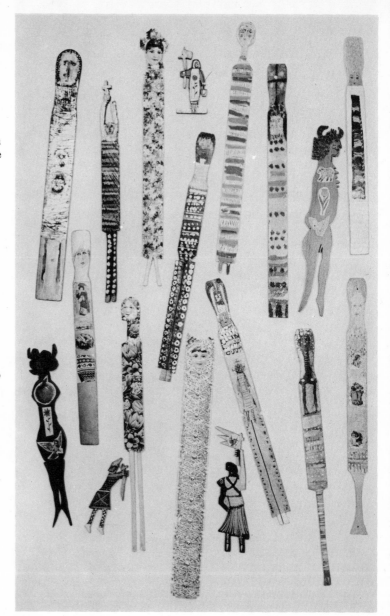

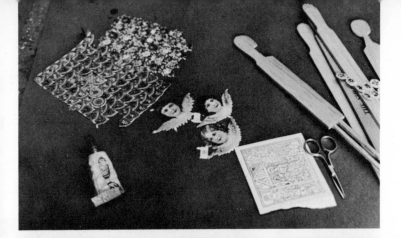

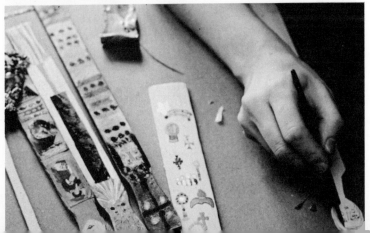

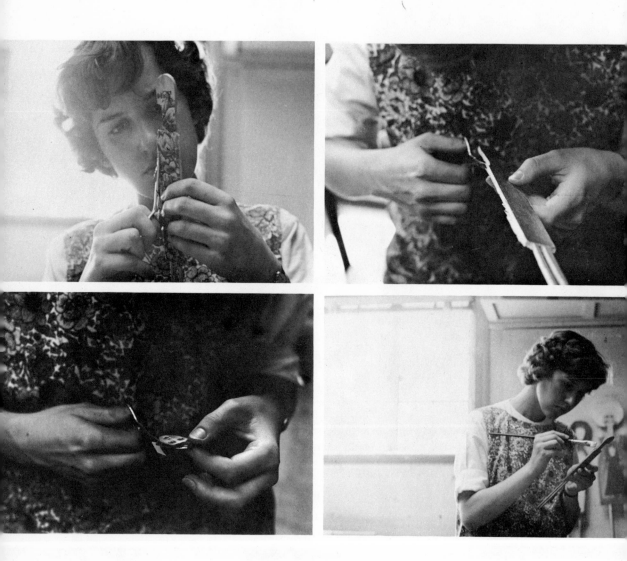

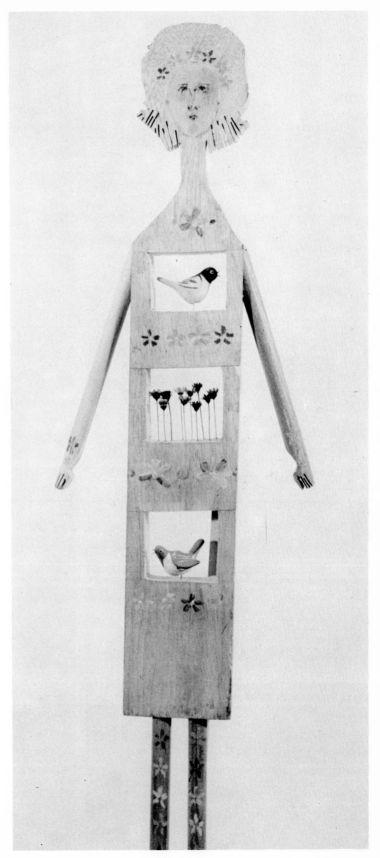

Anne Raymo

Anne Raymo

Project 11. Pick-up sticks.

Making giant-size pick-up sticks is particularly fun for young children. It teaches them how to design for a particular function — in this case, the sticks — and gives them something practical as well as beautiful. It also leads them to the realization that beauty need not be confined to formal works of art.

You will need dowels about one-half inch in diameter. Because these dowels are already finished, they need not be cut or sanded. However, plain dowels are not particularly attractive. They should be decorated.
If you are a teacher, you have two choices here. You may follow the exact rules of the game, in which case you will need basic colors to represent different points. The class may be divided into sections, each assigned to decorate sticks of a certain color. Or, you may allow each child to make his own stick in any fashion he chooses and let every stick be equal in point value. No matter which approach you choose, someone should make a black stick to help pick up the other sticks.

The sticks may be decorated with crayons, poster paints, inks, or whatever else is at hand. Little motifs cut from magazines and other small objects, such as sequins and string, can be pasted on the sticks. In fairness to the players, the sticks should have no protruding decor that might catch on other sticks during the game. The finished sticks may be coated with fixative to keep the design from rubbing off during the game.

Project 12. Totem poles and standards.

Surprisingly enough, large functional pieces of wood are quite cheap. Unpainted oars, for example, come sanded smooth and ready for decorating. The

rails for split rail fences, although more rustic, are finished enough to decorate. Oars and rails may be used to make standards for schools and classes or just to set up something amusing in the yard.

You may want to carve the oar or rail before painting it. This makes it a kind of skinny totem pole. The paint used depends on where the object will be displayed. If it is to remain permanently outdoors, use enamels and other outdoor paints. If it is to be kept indoors, you have a great choice in coloring agents.

Project 13. Wooden spoons.

Most dime stores sell unpainted wooden spoons in sets of three for about twenty-five cents. These spoons may be used to make dolls and stick figures or decorated for use in the kitchen or dining room. If the spoons are to be used with food, they should be varnished. Actually, painted spoons are more practical for serving dry foods. Salad spoons and similarly used spoons must be washed after each use, and frequent washings in detergents eventually corrode both varnish and design.

Project 14. Plates and bowls.

As you are shopping in the dime store for unpainted wooden spoons, you will probably come across unpainted plates and bowls. Why not decorate these too? They have greater surface on which to work and are thick enough to be carved and incised.

Again, what applies to decorated spoons in terms of care and use applies here. A painted plate should be varnished to project the design, and frequent washings in detergents should be avoided. For this reason, a decorated bowl is better used as a fruit dish than a salad bowl. Of course, if the bowl is simply incised or carved and not painted, it requires little special care.

Tray, carved with Scottish motifs, Rhode Island, 19th century. (Courtesy of the National Gallery of Art, Index of American Design, Washington.)

Butter Stamp, 19th century. (Courtesy of the National Gallery of Art, Index of American Design, Washington.)

Bill Greer

Project 15. Pictures mounted on wood.

Frequently you come across beautiful or appealing pictures in magazines or elsewhere that

may be presented on carved and gilded wood. Some subject matter, like many modern drawings, requires stark backings, others need more elaborate treatment. Another use for this project is the preservation and presentation of children's drawings for display. In the classroom, the children can make the mountings themselves, as part of their art projects.

deserve preservation. Here is a means of preserving such pictures, and frequently adding to their value by the handsome way in which they are presented: adhere them directly to wooden planks.

A flat plank larger than the picture may be stained, painted, or decorated with crayons to make a handsome backing for a picture. The picture should determine the kind of mounting. A Currier and Ives type print may be mounted on wood that has been stained and antiqued. (See Project 9.) A Gothic painting from an art magazine

Richie Kehl

There are two main methods of adhering a picture to wood. One is to simply spread glue all over the back of the picture and paste it on the wood, smoothing out the bumps. When the set-up is dry, the picture and wood may be brushed with varnish or sprayed with lacquer. Another way is to coat both the wood and the picture with white Liquitex,

a synthetic medium with good adhesive properties that dries clear. When the picture is mounted, Liquitex may be brushed over its face. This will provide a protective coat, and the picture may be cleaned later with a damp cloth without any damage to it.

Project 16. Unpainted furniture and doors.

Here are suggestions for the ambitious. If you have had any experience with design and painting on wood, you can probably make more distinctive looking furniture than that sold in the most exclusive decorator shops.

Today Early American, Modern, and almost any other style of furniture can be purchased unpainted. You can design something for the entire piece, or choose some part of the furniture, like the back of a chair, for decoration. Your design should suit the shape and style of the furniture, although departures from this rule can be startlingly successful.

If working first on paper, draw your design the size it will be and render it fairly carefully. You may even wish to cut it out and position it on the furniture with masking tape. Or, you may design directly on the furniture with chalk, which is easy to wipe off.

Doors are good surfaces on which to create large images for prominent display and practical use. You may paint a door already hung in your home, incorporating its glass panes, door knobs, and clothes' hooks as part of your image. Or, you may work with an unfinished door purchased at your local lumber yard for about ten dollars. The completed image may be used as a door, hung as a painting, or placed on legs and used as a table.

Chest from Berks Country, Pa., American, ca. 1780. (Courtesy of The Metropolitan Museum of Art, New York City, Rogers Fund, 1923.)

Dower Chest from Lancaster County, Pa., American, 18th century. (Courtesy of The Metropolitan Museum of Art, New York City, Gift of Mrs. Robert W. de Forest, 1933.)

Project 17. Mottos as plaques.

Most of us have favorite mottos or quotations. They may be patriotic, religious, romantic, or just plain nostalgic. Since these

front

sayings are ideas summarized in words, they are ready-made for another form of expression, the visual. They are ideal inspirations for plaques.

Plaques are flat wooden images used as ornaments on walls and furniture. You can paint, scratch, incise, or carve your plaque. You may nail things to it or paste things on it. You can probably think of a whole range of techniques suitable to your theme.

back

Intermediate Projects

The following projects are a little more sophisticated in concept and execution than the previous ones. Most of them require some basic familiarity with woodworking tools and

Bill Greer

Made in Japan

their uses. However, even a beginner can do these projects. As with most other things in life, the projects may seem difficult, but once you throw yourself into them, they resolve themselves more easily than originally expected.

Project 18. Puzzles.

Puzzles are fun to make and fun to do. Most wooden images, both two and three-dimensional, can be made into puzzles. For example, the pictures on wood suggested in Project 15 are ideal for making the familiar jigsaw puzzle. Once the picture is securely glued down and protected with some kind of coating, you can cut it. The complexity of the cuts depends on the subject matter and the age of the puzzle fan. The kind of saw available also determines

117

how complex the puzzle can be. Hand saws with broad blades, as discussed before, are good only for simple, straight cuts. More complex cuts can be made with the sabre saw, and very complex cuts with the coping saw.

Of course jigsaw puzzles are not the only kind of puzzle. Puzzles like the one pictured on page 17 are deceptive; they are harder to do than they look. To make circular cuts like those pictured on page 17 you will need a sabre saw, a narrow-bladed power saw that starts its own holes. Since the pieces should be as much alike in shape as possible in a puzzle of this kind, carving or drilling and sawing the holes is impractical.

One of the most complex puzzles is the three-dimensional puzzle with interlocking parts. These parts are quite difficult to plan and shape, so we suggest you fudge a little. Buy a cheap (about fifty cents) wooden puzzle with interlocking pieces and decorate it yourself.

Project 19. Ring-toss games.

To make a ring-toss game you will need a flat piece of wood, dowels or large cuphooks, and the rubber sealing rings used in home canning jars. The rubber rings are to be tossed onto the dowels or cuphooks.

You may use a square piece of wood, or shape the wood with a saw. The painted or incised design could include some kind of point system to make the game more exciting. Also, the design could incorporate the cuphooks or dowels. An obvious example is, if using dowels, to have painted birds perching on the dowels.

The choice of dowels or cuphooks to catch the rings depends on available tools. The dowels should be set into the flat piece of wood to prevent their tilting in the wrong direction or dropping off the backboard. To set the dowels, drill a hole slightly larger than the dowel and angle the hole so the dowel will tilt up. Then put glue on the dowel and insert it.

If you don't have the tools to set in the dowels, use cuphooks. These can be easily screwed into the backboard. If you have trouble inserting the cuphooks, make a hole first with a hammer and nail or an awl.

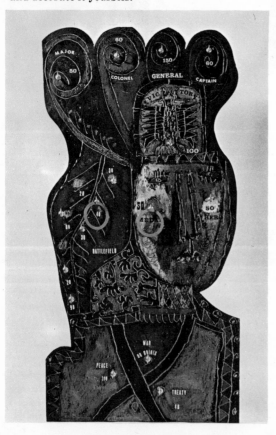

John Alcorn

Project 20. Peg the tail on the donkey.

Masonite, a composition board, comes in sheets with evenly punched holes, and golf tees or whittled sticks fit these holes. This happy coincidence may be exploited by the maker of wooden images. One obvious suggestion is to paint a donkey on the Masonite and make tails for the pegs. Designing a donkey or whatever other animal you select for the game might include using the ready-made holes as part of the design. The tails should be made of some light material so that the blindfolded player won't have to jam his peg or tee into the board in order to support the weight hanging from the peg. Balsa is a light wood that can be cut with a scissors and punched to hold a tee. Rope or the nylon swatches sold as "hair" pieces in dime stores can be glued onto the tee or whittled stick, or fabric may be used.

You can probably think of many other uses for Masonite pegboard. One fifth grade teacher had his students design a large map of the Civil War, with grey figures as Confederates mounted on one set of pegs and blue figures for Union troops mounted on another. The class followed the progress of the war by changing the positions and numbers of the participants.

Another teacher and class used the pegboard idea to explain atoms, molecules, ionization, and compounds. A first grade teacher and class used it to illustrate arithmetic. The results were beautiful as well as informative.

"Come Alive," Pepsi Cola.

Project 21. Dart Games.

The design of a dart game is controlled by which kind of darts are to be used: the sharp pointed ones or the rubber suction-cup darts. If the game is to be played indoors or by young children, the suction-cup darts obviously are desirable. Because sharp darts cover the face of the image with holes, you may wish to design something that would be enhanced by the antiqued look.

The rubber suction-cup darts do not, of course, mar the surface of the image. To make them stick to it, however, you need to coat the surface with at least four layers of varnish or cover the surface with Plexiglas. Plexiglas is a lightweight, transparent, non-reflecting plastic sheet. It can be purchased in lumber yards and at some glass supply and hardware stores. The shape of the Plexiglas should match that of the image. Square shapes are not difficult; have them cut to size when you buy them. If your image has an irregular outline, you can lay it on the Plexiglas, trace the outline with a crayon, and then cut it with a saw. The cut Plexiglas should be screwed onto the image. Drill holes in the Plexiglas through which to insert the screws.

Darts for the game are available at most hobby and toy stores. They may be thrown by hand, and the suction-cup darts may also be shot from special guns — a factor that may influence the subject matter of the images.

Project 22. Marble rolls.

Here is a game of skill enjoyed by young and old. Wood is a good material for making marble games because there are a few construction problems. First, the game needs sturdy sides to prevent the marbles from rolling off the board. Thin strips of wood can easily be nailed to the board to form sides. Second, the game needs holes deep enough to catch and hold the marbles. These holes can be quickly drilled in wood with either a hand or electric drill. Thus, the structural problems that might be difficult in paper, cardboard, metal, or some other material are easily solved in wood.

Project 23. Bean bag game.

Wooden images for bean bag games should be large, as they require holes big enough through which to throw the bags. These holes should be designed as part of the image, not just cut any old place. They need not be precise circles. Because the bean bag changes shape as it is thrown and upon impact, you may use triangular, oval, and circular holes. Of course, some holes — like the triangular ones — are harder to get a bag through. These could have a higher scoring value, if a point system is used.

Because the holes need not be precision cut, several tools may be used to cut them. The sabre saw is, of course, the ideal saw, but a jigsaw will also serve. Or, a chisel can be used to cut and shape the hole gradually.

The bean bags can be bought ready-made or made especially to match the game. The color of the bags is one obvious, and very handsome, way of complementing the image. Or, fabrics suitable to the theme of the image can be used. Dried peas or beans will serve for stuffing the bags. Incidentally, a bag with loosely packed beans is nicer to use and easier to get through the holes than a very full one.

Project 24. Blocks.

Blocks have been a neglected form of wooden images. This is unfortunate, because blocks designed and assembled numerous ways can be a real test for the imagination.

Blocks have six faces, and each can bear a part of a different image. The trick is to put the blocks together to form as many images as possible. Some faces may be interchangeable within the same image. Two, three, or up to 100 blocks can be used.

The number of blocks to be used determines to some extent their size. If only two or three blocks are used, they should be fairly large. Four inch cubes can be cut from a 4 x 4 inch redwood post. You can cut the post at home, although some cooperative lumber yards will do it for you. If numerous blocks are needed to form the image, precut children's wooden blocks, the kind you buy at dimestores, are ideal.

Richie Kehl

Advanced Projects

Now we are ready to approach projects more complex in concept and construction. As you read about them, you will see what we mean.

Project 25. Icons.

An icon is a form of portraiture that has something monumental about it. For example, a self-portrait is not an icon, but an image of the Virgin and Child may be. The maker of an icon usually feels quite strongly about his subject matter, and imparts to it a sense of majesty. He often chooses conventional poses and incorporates symbols in the image.

Because the maker of an icon is working under certain conceptual limitations, he must be imaginative enough to choose interesting materials and skillful enough in using them to make an image that is a highly personal interpretation of the subject matter, avoiding banality.

San Longino, probably made in New Mexico, 19th century. (Courtesy of the National Gallery of Art, Index of American Design, Washington.)

126

Project 26. Wooden puppets.

Puppets are a kind of Little People restricted to certain limited movements, always predictable, upon the pulling of a string. Puppet making and the uses of puppets in theater are topics so vast that we will confine ourselves here to puppets that can make only simple motions.

front

back

Refer to the puppet pictured on this page. The important consideration in making such a puppet is designing the movable parts so that they will be fairly lightweight and easy to manipulate. The parts should operate smoothly; otherwise a lot of strength is need to make them perform a simple motion. Notice that a nut, bolt, and washers are used for each joint. The bolt is inserted through a washer, then through the hole. Another washer is slipped over the bolt and the nut screwed on. The washers keep the nut and bolt from digging into the wood as they are moved. To prevent the strings from getting tangled, they can be run through eyelets screwed into the wood.

Project 27. Mobiles.

A mobile is a form of sculpture that has movable parts. These parts should be so constructed that they can easily be set in motion, even by a current of air. Naturally this poses problems, the main one being balance. The parts of a mobile, no matter how heavy they are, can be set in motion if they are properly balanced. Think of the playground seesaw. This is certainly no lightweight object, yet it can easily be moved by the slightest change in weight or brought to a dead standstill by unevenly distributed weight.

The seesaw operates on the lever principle. It is a rigid board that turns on one point, the fulcrum. The relationship of this point to the weight exerted on the ends of the seesaw is important. If two children of equal weight sit on each end, the seesaw balances if the fulcrum is dead center. If an adult sits on one end and a child on the other, the board should be moved so that the fulcrum is nearer the adult.

If you have never before made a mobile, we suggest you remember how the seesaw works and apply this idea to arranging the parts of your mobile. Even if your design has been carefully worked out on paper, you will need to re-adjust the positions of finished parts. Attach the objects to each end of the main dowel (or whatever you are using as a lever), and move this dowel on your finger until the objects balance one another. Mark this point, for from here you will suspend the next part of the mobile. Work out the balancing point of the next segment in the same way and connect the two levers. And so on, with all the segments.

If the levers still don't balance well, don't be too upset, for here wood once again comes to your aid. You can increase the weight of one object on each lever by pounding nails into it. The weight increase with each nail is so slight that you can gradually work to get the ideal weight distribution. Since nails come in such lovely forms as upholstery tacks, you can be increasing the surface ornamentation of the object as well as balancing the mobile.

Project 28. Wooden image clocks.

Thanks to modern technology and mass production, you can buy a cheap electric clock for about three dollars and incorporate it into a wooden image. The design possibilities for such an image are practically limitless. The hours may be marked with incised, chalked, or painted numbers or motifs. The face of the clock can be as formal or as frivolous as you desire. The problem in making a wooden image clock involves the clock itself. First and foremost, unplug the clock; you can get a nasty shock if you touch the wrong parts. Then remove the watchglass, hands, face, and box to reveal the clockworks. The clockworks are the basic unit to be incorporated into the image. Fit the bar which bore the hands through a hole drilled in the face of the image, then fasten the clockworks to the wood. Put the hands back on; plug the clock in, and call yourself a clockmaker.

Project 29. Decorated machines.

Attics, backyards, garages, and junk yards usually have machines or parts of machines that are beautiful. Divorced from their functional identity, they become sculptures with integrated planes, angles, and surface interest. However, it takes an artist to see this and an artist to capitalize on it.

Many machines have removable parts that can be replaced with something in wood. The images on these wooden inserts may emphasize some aspects of the machine or facetiously depart from them. Your design will probably reflect how you feel about machines generally.

Project 30. Story telling.

One of the most rewarding uses of wooden images is making a small theater and characters to tell a story. Almost everybody enjoys this, and it is particularly thrilling for young children. They can get involved in all aspects of it, from creating a story to making the backdrops and participants in the story.

This is a long-term project for an individual, but a class should be able to do it in a few weeks. The problems of doing such a project are suggested in the photographic sequence of our own story. It is a simple fairy tale: boy meets girl, problems develop, boy gets girl, and everybody lives happily ever after.

Liz King, St. Mary's College, Notre Dame, Indiana.

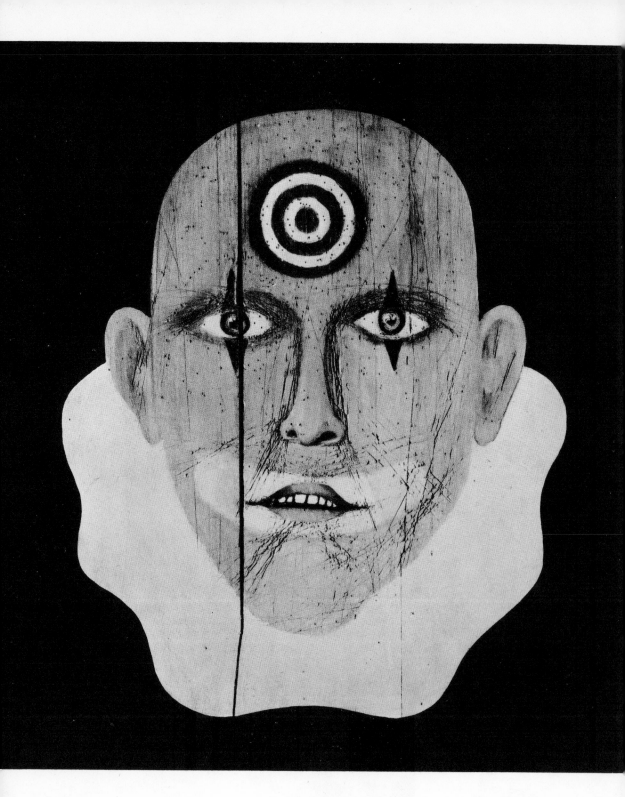

ACKNOWLEDGMENTS

A book of this kind is a cooperative effort, and the authors relied heavily on the help of many people and institutions.

Our thanks to the artists who contributed their work: William Accorsi, Holly Carpenter, Paul Davis, Karen Eisin, Walter Einsell, Milton Glaser, Bill Greer, Richie Kehl, Susan Ocock, Anne Raymo, and Tomi Ungerer.

Some of the institutions that allowed perusal of their collections include the New York Historical Society, the Cooper Union Museum, the Museum of Modern Art, the Metropolitan Museum of Art, and the Museum of Early American Folk Art — all of New York City — and the National Gallery of Art, Washington, D.C. We are particularly grateful to Lina Abt, of The Index of American Design, who cooperated with us above and beyond the call of duty. Also, thanks to George Beylerian of Scarabaeus, Ltd., New York City, who trustingly lent us several valuable objects to be photographed.

To the photographer Dick Olsen, who patiently waited for us to pose the art work, our appreciation. To Neal Beitzel, who photographed several dolls; to Harry Calahan, who photographed the nature study scenes; and to Thecla, who photographed the images that appeared in the Pepsi Cola "Come Alive" exhibit, our thanks. To Jim Cronin and the rest of the staff of del Sol Productions, Ossining, New York, who stepped over and around piles of photographs and manuscript, our thanks. And special thanks to Gail Prosser, who helped us meet our deadline by supplying us with transfusions of black coffee.

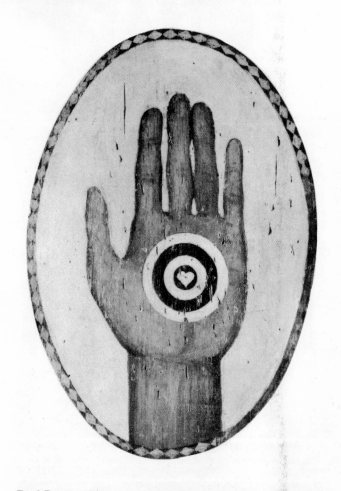

Paul Davis. (Courtesy of Push Pin Studios, New York City.)